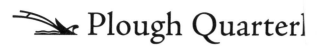 

Plough Quarterly

BREAKING GROUND FOR A RENEWED WORLD

Spring 2017, Number 12

Artists: Nikolay Nikolayevich Ge, Boris Ivanovich Kopylov, Taisia Afonina, Wayne Forte, Julian Peters, Jason Landsel, Dave Beckerman, Luca Sartoni, Wu Guanzhong, Sadao Watanabe

Cover: The girl and balloon were painted by Banksy on a Southbank wall in London, with the words, "There is always hope." See photo on page 3.

WWW.PLOUGH.COM

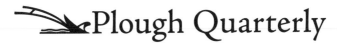

Plough Quarterly

WWW.PLOUGH.COM

Meet the community behind *Plough*.

Plough Quarterly is published by the Bruderhof, an international community of people seeking to follow Jesus together. Members of the Bruderhof are committed to a way of radical discipleship in the spirit of the Sermon on the Mount. Inspired by the first church in Jerusalem (Acts 2 and 4), members renounce private property and share everything in common in a life of service to God, one another, and neighbors near and far.

The community includes families and single people from a wide range of backgrounds, with around 2,700 people in all. There are twenty-three Bruderhof settlements in both rural and urban locations in the United States, England, Germany, Australia, and Paraguay.

To learn more or arrange a visit, see the community's website at *bruderhof.com.*

Plough Quarterly features original stories, ideas, and culture to inspire everyday faith and action. Starting from the conviction that the teachings and example of Jesus can transform and renew our world, we aim to apply them to all aspects of life, seeking common ground with all people of goodwill regardless of creed. The goal of *Plough Quarterly* is to build a living network of readers, contributors, and practitioners so that, in the words of Hebrews, we may "spur one another on toward love and good deeds."

Plough Quarterly includes contributions that we believe are worthy of our readers' consideration, whether or not we fully agree with them. Views expressed by contributors are their own and do not necessarily reflect the editorial position of *Plough* or of the Bruderhof communities.

Editors: Peter Mommsen, Sam Hine, Maureen Swinger. Art director: Emily Alexander. Online editor: Erna Albertz.
Founding Editor: Eberhard Arnold (1883–1935).
Plough Quarterly No. 12: Courage
Published by Plough Publishing House, ISBN 978-0-87486-135-8
Copyright © 2017 by Plough Publishing House. All rights reserved.

Scripture quotations (unless otherwise noted) are from the New Revised Standard Version Bible, copyright © 1989 the Division of Christian Education of the National Council of the Churches of Christ in the United States of America. Used by permission. All rights reserved. Front cover and page 3: Photograph of Banksy image by Kathy deWitt / Alamy Stock Photo. Inside front cover: Wikimedia Commons (public domain). Back cover: *Saint Francis and the Birds* © 2017 Watanabe Sadao | Eyekons.

Editorial Office
PO Box 398
Walden, NY 12586
T: 845.572.3455
info@plough.com

Subscriber Services
PO Box 345
Congers, NY 10920-0345
T: 800.521.8011
subscriptions@plough.com

United Kingdom
Brightling Road
Robertsbridge
TN32 5DR
T: +44(0)1580.883.344

Australia
4188 Gwydir Highway
Elsmore, NSW
2360 Australia
T: +61(0)2.6723.2213

Plough Quarterly (ISSN 2372-2584) is published quarterly by Plough Publishing House, PO Box 398, Walden, NY 12586.
Individual subscription $32 per year in the United States; Canada add $8, other countries add $16.
Periodicals postage paid at Walden, NY 12586 and at additional mailing offices.
POSTMASTER: Send address changes to *Plough Quarterly,* PO Box 345, Congers, NY 10920-0345.

A Time for Courage

Dear Reader,

It's proving to be an unsettling year. Words such as "crisis," "resistance," and "collapse" pepper headlines, and few dismiss them as mere alarmism. All is not well – on this, at least, there is broad consensus. The political cultures of Western countries are infested with rage. Cold War nightmares such as nuclear conflict are suddenly again imaginable. On the five-hundredth anniversary of the Reformation, Christian denominations – far from nearing a grand restoration of unity – find themselves riven by half-hidden schisms. Partisan divisions infect private life, hardening barriers and poisoning friendships.

At such a moment, being told to "take courage" can sound like a grim joke. No doubt that's how it sounded to the friends of Jesus who accompanied him on his last journey to Jerusalem, where he would be killed. Yet, as John reports in the sixteenth chapter of his Gospel, "Take courage!" was one of the last things Jesus told his disciples, just hours before his arrest and execution. He added, in a statement that must have puzzled them: "I have overcome the world."

Courage – *heart,* etymologically – seems to me precisely what we're in need of today: courage to stand by the truth, and courage to stand by the gospel's claim that everyone belongs to God, because Jesus has overcome the world. Such courage, according to Augustine, is simply a form of love – "love ready to bear all things for God's sake."

To inspire such love – and to guard against a failure of nerve or of imagination – this issue of *Plough* highlights lived examples of the virtue of courage. This can take the form of boldness in the face of persecution, as shown by Yu Jie's firsthand account of the challenges facing the church in China (page 30). It can be the bold decision taken by police officer Steven McDonald to forgive the young shooter who paralyzed him, and to spend the rest of his life testifying to the power of forgiveness (page 10). Courage is the willingness of a family and a community to affirm that a young man with severe disabilities was born for a missionary purpose, contrary to the utilitarian creed of our times, as Maureen Swinger recounts (page 18).

A synonym for courage favored by the apostle Paul is *perseverance.* Few have persevered as tirelessly as Dorothy Day, a social-justice radical in the best sense, who gave herself daily in unspectacular acts of love. What was exceptional about Day was her consistency in living out the hard demands of the gospel. Readings from *The Reckless Way of Love,* a new book from *Plough,* reveal the source of the inner strength that allowed Day to do so without burning out (page 50).

As dangerous as the temptation is to become disheartened in a year like this, there is a danger more insidious still: the voice whispering that despite the suffering and degradation around us *it's not really that bad.* This voice, of course, is far more likely to speak to the comfortable and affluent than to refugees, poor immigrants, the incarcerated, or the starving. It is also more likely to speak to those who believe that Christianity is doing just fine – that, setting aside a few inevitable shortcomings, we Christians have no urgent need to repent, certainly not in a way that would visibly transform our everyday lives.

A new book by Rod Dreher, *The Benedict Option,* has been garnering attention – and much of it amounts to a howl of protest against Dreher's call for Christians to strategically retreat from seeking cultural power in order to build stronger Christian communities. (See *Plough's* interview with Dreher in our last issue, as well as the thoughtful letters in "Readers Respond" on page 5.) Dreher's various proposals can certainly be constructively criticized. But many reactions, it seems to me, altogether ignore his book's basic insight: that Western churches, virtually across the board, have failed to cultivate faithful discipleship within a post-Christian culture. The symptoms of this failure are well documented, and damning. They include our ineffectiveness in passing the faith on to the next generation, as shown by sociologists such as Christian Smith;

We need the courage to dare tangible changes in our lives.

the extent to which materialism and consumerism – and militarism and nationalism – have polluted our everyday lives; divorce rates as high among Christians as among others; and an epidemic of pornography addiction afflicting Christian men.

In the face of these alarming facts, it is not enough to simply cry, "No withdrawal from culture!" while quoting the Great Commission. If we Christians do not show forth the justice and faithfulness of the kingdom of God in the way we live, why should anyone pay attention to our preaching? And isn't it obvious that our response to these ills – or rather, our repentance for our sins – must include pouring far more energy into building church communities in which children are educated in the faith, mutual care is a priority, accountability to the church is really practiced, and economic sharing ensures that no brother or sister is in material need? That doesn't sound like a retreat to me. It sounds like simply doing what the New Testament tells us to do: bear one another's burdens, watch over one another's souls, love one another.

We need courage, then, to see our Christianity with honest eyes – and to dare the tangible changes in our lives that the Spirit may then direct us to make. We'll find this courage when we learn to see the world as God sees it. Jesus has overcome the world, and everyone in it belongs to him, even if many still resist him for the time being. This is the hope that Christoph F. Blumhardt points us to (page 56): hope for every human being and for all creation, because Jesus is victor.

Warm greetings,

Peter

Peter Mommsen
Editor

Kingdom Politics

On William H. Willimon's "Alien Citizens":
This article walks a thin line between witness and quietism. Church *is* God's answer to politics, but it must also confront the world with the life of Christ. We cannot curl up in our congregations and stick to our knitting until we magically get it right. We have to take our Christianity out into the streets and bang it against the world until the parts that don't look like Jesus break and fall off. Our witness will often fail, will doubtless be mocked and pitied, just as the author recounts, but as someone once said, it is not our job to win, it is our job to be faithful. Winning is God's job, and he will do it in his own time. Until then a truly faithful church will certainly attend to building its members in faith, but the works that will give life to that faith will involve radical, forceful confrontation with "the powers that be."

Brian Dolge

If this had been the ecclesial vision of Dr. Martin Luther King, Jr. and others in the black church, there never would have been a civil rights movement. It's precisely because we have a generation of preachers who "eschew commentary on current events" in light of the gospel message that the church makes no noticeable difference today in the life of the world. . . .

There are insights from Dietrich Bonhoeffer's monumental *Ethics,* published posthumously, that run counter to the framework set forth by Willimon and Stanley Hauerwas. Bonhoeffer was executed because of his part in plans to act directly on the state to stop the perpetration of evil – even as we must do, where called for, contra the claims of Willimon that we act by being some sort of model community. As Bonhoeffer noted, "the first demand which is made of those who belong to God's church is not that they should be something in themselves, not that they should, for example, set up some religious organization or that they should lead lives of piety, but that

they shall be witnesses to Jesus Christ before the world. It is for this task that the Holy Spirit equips those to whom he gives himself." Willimon's lofty and poetic prose sounds rapt, until you get to the end and realize you actually have nothing that "sticks" – like trying to pin Jell-O to the wall.

Susanne Johnson, Dallas, TX

Untitled,
Boris
Ivanovich
Kopylov

Willimon's article is not political in a sense that he wants you to be against Trump. Rather, he is calling for the church and especially the preachers to start being faithful to God *first* in the church through preaching the gospel and discipleship. It is through preaching and through the church that true Christ-followers are formed, such as those from Mother Emanuel Church in Charleston. The problem is not primarily Trump or the government system; it is the current church's failure to be faithful to God. God wants people to be saved, and that means preaching the real Word of God, not our personal agendas, self-help, or poor theology.

Willimon once again reminds us not to get distracted but to focus, focus, focus on Jesus Christ. When we truly follow Jesus, the Holy Spirit will transform us individually and as a church, and through the Holy Spirit's work in us, through us, and to others, the world will see who our Almighty God truly is. I just wonder how many Christians in America are ready for such a mighty move of the Holy Spirit.

Joseph Yang, New York, NY

Will Willimon responds: Quietism? Wow. That's the first time I've been charged with that anathema to Wesleyans (like me). Hey, I'm the guy who sued the governor and legislature of Alabama over their stupid anti-immigration law. And I won in court! I'm also doing everything I can to send our current president back to casino management and tax evasion. In my article, as Joseph Yang says, I'm trying to remind us that Christian politics is more radical than the most radical of leftist politics. In the present hour, we must keep reminding ourselves that Jesus Christ is Lord and the president is not.

Debating the Benedict Option

On *"Building a Communal Church: An Interview with* Benedict Option *author Rod Dreher"*: Dreher's descriptions of the kinds of intentional Christian communities necessary in our current situation point squarely at the needed reform of pastoral thinking and practice as well as parish life. It's time for a great awakening. My wife and I have participated in a community of the Neocatechumenal Way for nearly twenty-three years. Our experience corresponds directly to Dreher's described option. We have experienced the deep renewal that comes from a purposeful, missionary Christian life. We have seen its fruits in our children and the lives of others in our parish communities. It's no secret. I wholeheartedly concur with Dreher's calls for dramatic changes rooted in authentic conversion. Devotion to the status quo is a paralyzing force in the church, and whole families are perishing because of it. We can no longer pretend that "it's not like that here." It is very much like that here, there, and everywhere.   *Bill Beckman, Omaha, NE*

I read the article with great anticipation, excited by the title. I was very disappointed. Dreher's point of view is so mired in his politics that I frankly felt a bit soiled by the end. Although he ardently denies it, his approach is withdrawal from the world, the building of a fortress community, a bubble where we don't have to deal with ideas other than ours. Many of God's beloved children are clearly left out of his community. This is right-wing puritanism without praxis. I ardently look for an article that focuses on true community rather than the old "fortress for the saints."   *John Jackman, Winston-Salem, NC*

As a Benedictine, this is the first piece I have read that addresses the Benedictine way of life from a Protestant Fundamentalist point of view. Although some communities are cloistered, many of us see far more value in being the presence of Christ in society, rather than secluded from it. One of our prayers entreats God to "make me your other self." How can that be done when we separate ourselves from the world around us? I am much more drawn to the way of Jesus, who was willing to take the risk of being present even to those he knew would ultimately murder him.

Will Byrd, San Francisco, CA

I appreciate the editors' providing a broad range of ideas and enjoyed the Winter 2017 issue, my first. However, Dreher's broad, general opinions on what others should be doing and thinking, sadly, seemed arrogant, given his frequent admissions of so many occasions on which he has been misguided ("wrong," "arrogant agnostic," "never really stopped to think," "scared to death and allowed myself to be manipulated by the government").

Dreher's unsubstantiated allegation that there is a push to deny licenses to Canadian doctors who won't perform euthanasia is alarmist. In Canada there is currently no requirement in the law that doctors provide medical assistance in dying. The Canadian Medical Association supports the right of all physicians to follow their conscience in this matter. Exaggerations and misleading stories abound in public life today. In my opinion, they do nothing to persuade others to sound policy, primarily because they prevent serious discussion of tough issues and badly erode trust. Difficult situations do require us, even Christians, to openly and honestly discuss facts in order to make good decisions. I don't believe God will judge humanity by what the loudest and most opinionated of us thinks today. Can we agree to show more humility and allow our fellow Christians to try their best to follow the Lord's teaching?

Katharine A. Daly, Dunbarton, NH

Can someone involved in a sin that is not recognized as sin still be loved by the church? Is this not the question facing the sexual confusion today? At what point does the faith community discipline its members through grace and mercy? These are important questions. If we are not mutually dependent and committed in a community, how can we believe we have been given the "right" of discipline? The expectation of the current "church" is not of family but of pep rally. All we want is to feel good and be happy. If you are not happy where you are, find a "church" with better entertainment and nicer bathrooms.

Mark Smith, North Wales, PA

I was involved in evangelical Christianity, as it came to be known, in the eighties and nineties. People thought they did have authentic conversions. The proof was that they were evangelical about their faith. They were bold in their pronouncements. They were supposed to be the church that is being called for in this article. The spread of Christian-based schools exploded during this time. Isolating people in the schools doesn't seem to have worked. Now, the call is not just for schools, but live-in communities are required to protect our souls.

Margaret Collins, Springdale, PA

I wanted to like this idea: Thomas Merton and the radical actions of monks in community, something to challenge the zeitgeist of materialism and selfishness. A Christian movement to reimagine community in a brutalizing world. Rescuing Christianity from the political anger of Evangelicals. Instead it seems to me a pretty conservative and reactionary response to the modern world. "Why would we not embrace the sexual constructs and mores of first-century Jews?" the author asks. Hmm – along with slavery, etc.? . . . We should go forward to Christ, not return to something that is safe and self-satisfying.

Harry Robert Harper, Santa Cruz, CA

Dreher seems to have a very dualistic view of things, which cannot bring healing to the great divides that we face. As a Benedictine oblate, I find that he misunderstands the transformative reality of the actual Benedict Option. The monastics I know are deeply transformed people who do not lose their connections to, or concern for, the rest of society. They are savvy, informed, and incarnationally involved. Dreher seems to want to reinforce and protect a narrow understanding of certainty and morality, whereas true contemplative communities are uncomfortably transformative. You have to "die" to what you think you know.

Ellen Haroutunian, Lakewood, CO

Yes, we need to be part of a community of Christ's disciples to be formed in his image, but that is intended to give us the base from which we can reach out to a lost world. When Christians only show practical love to their own, they are not only unfaithful to the example and teaching of Jesus (Luke 6:32–36), but run the risk of creating "rice Christians," who have no real allegiance to Jesus but falsely profess faith for what they can get. All of society needs to be reconfigured, and that means being involved in politics.

Since I retired from the pastorate, my wife and I have moved to a church-plant on a local social housing estate. Here we share fellowship with folk who love the Lord and pray with real honesty and faith, but who know great deprivation. Those of us who are able try to provide food and clothing for those who need it. This is about as close to Acts 2 and 4 that we can practically achieve in our circumstances. Our pastor also runs the only free youth club in the area, giving youngsters an alternative to gang culture.

While it would be lovely to imagine our church families moving out to a nice Christian community in the country, that is not going to happen, not least because the jobs are here in the city. Many poorly paid Christians here are doing work to which they feel called by God. If we are a community in Christ's image, we are here for others, not just ourselves.

Your small Bruderhof community in London is a better model. Churches could develop communal living to make better use of available accommodation. Even secular friends recognize the need to develop cooperative housing.

Bob Allaway, London, UK

Rod Dreher responds: Some of these letters repeat a familiar experience I've had when I introduce the Benedict Option: people respond with anger and fear to what they imagine I am saying, instead of what I actually say. Will Byrd imagines that I am a fundamentalist Protestant who wants to retreat to a "fortress." I am an Eastern Orthodox believer who lives in the heart of the city – Bob Allaway, please note this. As is clear from any fair-minded reading of my interview, I believe we small-o orthodox Christians – Protestant, Catholic, and Eastern Orthodox – have to have some sort of limited separation from the world for the sake of formation, precisely so that we can be who Christ commands us to be for the world. Ellen Haroutunian ignores my plain, explicit words in the *Plough* interview, in which I said that we lay Christians cannot afford to live as cloistered monastics, and that I do not advocate heading for the hills. I do wonder why some people are so deathly afraid of any kind of countercultural way of Christian living.

As to the euthanasia situation in Canada, physicians currently have conscience protection, but there is a strong movement among euthanasia advocates, particularly within Canada's medical community, to compel doctors to "at a minimum" (the words of a federal advisory panel) refer patients seeking assisted suicide to physicians who will perform it. The federal panel also recommends that all "publicly-funded health care institutions" provide euthanasia upon request. Given Canada's single-payer health care system, that would mean that religiously run nursing homes and hospices could be compelled to facilitate euthanasia. As of this writing, conscience protections remain in place, but Canadian health-care workers to whom I have talked do not expect them to remain for much longer.

Not Our Wendell Berry

On Tamara Hill Murphy's "The Hole in Wendell Berry's Gospel":

Murphy suggests Wendell Berry's fiction provides a sort of Currier & Ives picture of life: all brightness and no blight. She also suggests there is not enough of the gospel in his work. In his nonfiction, at least, two ideas are central: first, that we have an obligation to care for God's creation, and second, that we are called to live in community. These ideas echo, respectively, Genesis and the second great commandment. As a Christian, I find this enough from an author.

Jim Severance, Loganville, WI

Any disagreement with Berry should begin with a fair reading of his work – otherwise one is simply battling a straw man. In this respect, I am afraid that even though Murphy agrees with much of Berry's vision, her essay misrepresents his fiction, claiming that his stories view rural life too nostalgically, glossing over its violence and racism and brokenness. . . . I've recently been

(Continued on page 75)

At the March For Life

Trevor Wiser

Vice President Pence's attendance at the March for Life created a lot of hype about the event this January, but that wasn't why my wife and I traveled to Washington, DC, to participate. We came to find out what being pro-life means to individuals in this movement.

We learned that the phrase is gaining new meaning for many young people across the nation. The talk from the stage may have been all about legislation, but on the ground in the crowd, people we spoke with were far more enthused about their work to support mothers and children. Few people would disagree that more needs to be done for our most vulnerable, but actually doing it takes work and sacrifice. We met the staff of crisis pregnancy centers, people from adoption agencies, and sidewalk counselors.

One young woman told us of a friend who was under intense pressure from her boyfriend to abort the child they had conceived. Conflicted, she called her youth leader, who connected her with some of the many organizations available to assist women in her situation. She kept the child, who is now doing well. The story epitomizes the spirit of the march: the rank and file of this movement is most concerned with lives, not legislation. The self-sacrifice and dedication of the people we met give us hope for a day when abortion really is unthinkable.

One great resource for this new generation of pro-lifers is *Life Matters Journal,* a nonsectarian, nonpartisan magazine addressing many forms of violence – not only abortion but also war, capital punishment, euthanasia, torture, and embryonic stem cell research.

lifemattersjournal.org

Why the Death Penalty Must Die

American Christians are largely responsible for the continued existence of the death penalty in their country, according to Shane Claiborne's book *Executing Grace: How the Death Penalty Killed Jesus and Why It's Killing Us.* Claiborne and others, including Cynthia Vaughn *(right),* who forgave her father on death row for murdering her mother; Stacy

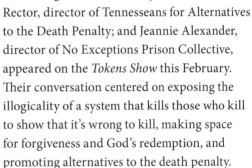

Rector, director of Tennesseans for Alternatives to the Death Penalty; and Jeannie Alexander, director of No Exceptions Prison Collective, appeared on the *Tokens Show* this February. Their conversation centered on exposing the illogicality of a system that kills those who kill to show that it's wrong to kill, making space for forgiveness and God's redemption, and promoting alternatives to the death penalty.

For decades now, *Plough* has partnered with members of Murder Victims' Families for Reconciliation to bring the voices of victims' families into the public conversation. MVFR advocates for ending the death penalty and promotes restorative justice as the best way to heal the damage caused by violence and to create a safer, more compassionate, and more just society.

mvfr.org

Poet in This Issue: Christopher Zimmerman Zimmerman, a Bruderhof pastor and contributing editor to *Plough,* wrote the poems in this issue during the years he lived at the community's Harlem House in New York City. He now serves at the Holzland community in Thuringia, Germany. ➤

Top, Participants in the March for Life in Washington, DC, January 27, 2017

Bottom, Cynthia Vaughn forgave her father on death row for murdering her mother.

DETECTIVE STEVEN MCDONALD of the New York City Police Department, who died January 10, was shot in the line of duty in 1986 and paralyzed from the neck down. Confined to a wheelchair and dependent on a ventilator to breathe, he forgave his teenage assailant.

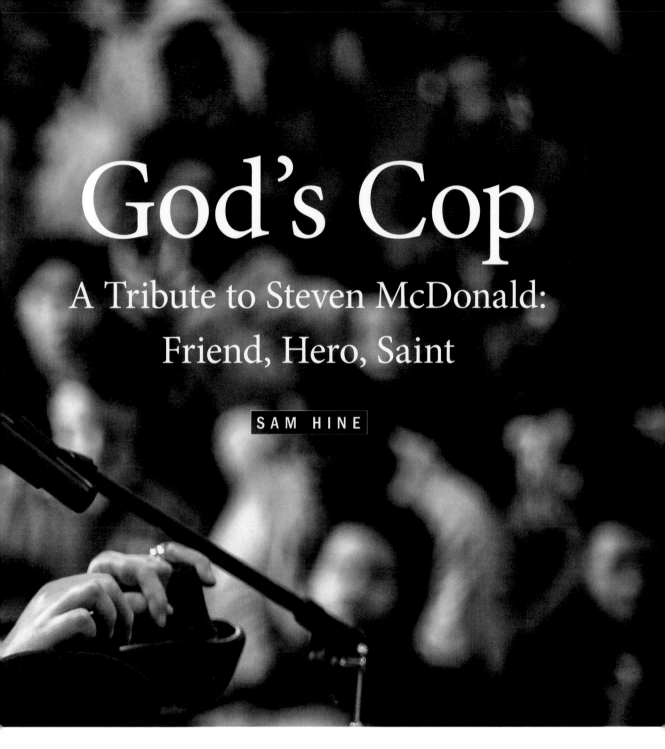

God's Cop

A Tribute to Steven McDonald: Friend, Hero, Saint

SAM HINE

I first met Steven McDonald in the studio of a national TV talk show. The night before, a young black man, Malcolm Ferguson, had been shot and killed by police in the Bronx after protesting the acquittal of four police officers in the shooting death of unarmed immigrant Amadou Diallo in the same neighborhood. Tensions between police and the black

Steven McDonald addressing high school students in the Bronx in 2006

Sam Hine is an editor at Plough. ▶ *Watch Steven McDonald at* plough.com/stevenmcdonald.

Steven McDonald, his wife Patti Ann, and son Conor in March 2015

community had skyrocketed. Could anyone bridge that chasm or at least close the distance? Or would a third-generation Irish-Catholic NYPD officer who had been shot point-blank by a black teenager pour gas on the fire?

I needn't have worried. McDonald was there to promote a new book, *Why Forgive?*, in which his friend, Bruderhof pastor Johann Christoph Arnold, tells McDonald's story. Joining him was Roberto Rodriguez, a victim of police brutality in Los Angeles who is also featured in *Why Forgive?* Radiating peace as they calmly recounted their stories, the two men acknowledged the need for justice but offered a more radical prescription for the healing of individual souls and entire cities: forgiveness and prayer.

Speaking in bursts between the puffs of his breathing machine, McDonald said, "Many people of different races and different religions were praying for me to live when I was dying, which I was. And when I was told that I would be completely disabled, they prayed that I would recover my abilities. I believe God answered that prayer in giving me the faith and love to forgive the young man who shot me."

> **❝** The only thing worse than a bullet in my spine would have been revenge in my heart."

On July 12, 1986, McDonald, a twenty-nine-year-old police officer on patrol in Central Park, stopped to question three teenagers about a recent bicycle theft. The oldest, a fifteen-year-old, took out a gun and shot him in the head, neck, and arm. McDonald was rushed to a hospital, where surgeons told his wife that he would be paralyzed from the neck down for the rest of his life. He later wrote:

My wife, twenty-three years old, was three months pregnant. Patti Ann was crying uncontrollably at the cards she had been dealt, and I cried too. I was locked in my body, unable to speak, move, or reach out to her.

A week after I was shot, the media asked to speak to my wife. Though still in shock, Patti Ann bravely told everybody that she would trust God to do what was best for her family. That set the tone not only for my recovery but also for the rest of our lives.

McDonald spent the next eighteen months in hospital. Six months after the shooting, Patti Ann gave birth to their son, Conor. At Conor's baptism, McDonald publicly forgave Shavod Jones, the teen who had shot him.

I wanted to free myself of all the negative, destructive emotions that this act of violence awoke in me – the anger, the bitterness, the hatred. I needed to free myself of those so I could be free to love my wife and our child and those around us. I often tell people that the only thing worse than a bullet in my spine would have been to nurture revenge in my heart. Such an attitude would have extended my tragic injury into my soul, hurting my wife, son, and others even more. It is bad enough that the physical effects are permanent, but at least I can choose to prevent spiritual injury.

> **" God has turned something terrible into something beautiful."**

A year or two later, Jones called the McDonalds from prison and apologized. McDonald hoped that someday the two of them could travel the country together, sharing the story of the terrible day that changed the course of both their lives. In 1995, Jones was released from prison. Three days later he died in a motorcycle accident. But as McDonald would often say, "Shavod Jones is with me wherever my story is told. We have helped many people, the two of us."

I know it may be hard to understand, but I would rather be like this and feel the way I do, than go on living like I was before. Of course, I have my ups and downs. Some days, when I am not feeling well, I get angry. I get depressed. There have been times when I even felt like killing myself. But I have come to realize that anger is a wasted emotion. So I forgive that young man all over again, and every time I tell my story, I think of Shavod, and I forgive him.

Months and years have come and gone, and I've never regretted forgiving Shavod. Back then we never imagined it would carry any importance in other people's lives. We did

Top, McDonald was taken to Bellevue Hospital after the shooting.

Bottom, The aftermath: McDonald, now paralyzed, as a young father

Johann Christoph Arnold, Steven McDonald, and students from Lawrence Road Middle School, New York, in 2008

it for ourselves. But ever since, people have wanted to hear about this act of forgiveness. It helped us, but more importantly it has helped others as well.

In the wake of the Columbine High School shooting in 1999, McDonald and Arnold joined forces to launch a program called Breaking the Cycle, bringing a message of nonviolent conflict resolution through forgiveness to assemblies at New York–area schools.

I've been able to reach out to children in particular, because it was a child of my city that did this terrible thing to me. I have spoken at hundreds of

schools about nonviolence, and I know from responses I get that many of the children have embraced my message and internalized it. Instead of responding to violence with more violence they have decided to choose forgiveness and love. So God has turned something terrible into something beautiful.

> **"**Lord, make me an instrument of your peace."

A quintessential Irishman and Catholic, McDonald asked Arnold, a Protestant, to help him bring their message of healing through

In 2005, McDonald brought his message of forgiveness to the Holy Land. Visiting the Sea of Galilee, he asked his caregivers to remove his shoes and place his feet in the water.

forgiveness to Northern Ireland. The Good Friday Agreement had recently been effected, ending decades of open conflict, but the wounds were still raw and deep. With "marching season" tensions simmering and police in armored vehicles and riot gear standing by, the two men accompanied a children's chorus up Garvaghy Road and through other volatile neighborhoods, prayed together in Protestant and Catholic churches, listened to victims of violence on both sides, and addressed members of Parliament at Stormont.

Accompanying them was Franciscan priest Mychal Judge, the New York Fire Department chaplain who would become the first recorded fatality at the World Trade Center on September 11, 2001, where he had gone to minister to the wounded. That day scuttled the three men's plans to bring their work for reconciliation to the Middle East. Four years later McDonald and Arnold made the trip, meeting with Jewish and Palestinian bereaved parents, police, and human rights activists.

> **"**I would do it again even if I knew what was going to happen."

World leaders, celebrities, and millions of ordinary people have drawn inspiration from the McDonalds' story. And who can deny that it was their witness to faithfulness in marriage, come what may, that so stirred and challenged us? Last December, Patti Ann, now the mayor of Malverne, New York, joined Steven on stage at a school assembly. Looking back over their thirty-one years of marriage, she told the students, "We were married eight months when Steven was shot. People ask me if I was to do it all over again, would I do it, and I say yes. I would do it again even if I knew what was going to happen." Steven responded, "I'm very blessed to have had this time with Patti Ann. I think I never understood or appreciated how beautiful, wonderful, and great an experience it would be to share a life with someone else. It's been life-giving without any end. Without

NYPD officers await McDonald's casket outside New York's Saint Patrick's Cathedral on January 13, 2017.

Patti Ann in my life, I wouldn't be here today, I wouldn't be speaking on these very important issues, I wouldn't be alive."

Steven McDonald's life ended on January 10, four days after a heart attack left him in a coma. Thousands of New Yorkers packed Saint Patrick's Cathedral and the streets outside to pay their respects at his funeral Mass, which Timothy Cardinal Dolan officiated. Mayor Bill de Blasio said McDonald showed us that "the work of policing is profoundly based on love and compassion for your fellow man and woman" and must be guided by Jesus' greatest commandments: to love God and to love your neighbor as yourself. "Brothers and sisters, we all watched Steven live out these commandments. That message from the gospel governed his life, a message centuries and centuries old that he made fresh and real for us all."

Conor McDonald, now an NYPD sergeant, recounted how his father would call him every day at 5:00 a.m. while he patrolled, just to

At one of his last school assemblies, at the Mount Academy in Esopus, New York, Steven McDonald said:

> People want to know: How did you forgive the young man who shot you? And again, looking back, pondering on my life since that time, it's clear to me that God was in charge. All he wanted was the opportunity to use me. He just needed my yes, and that was made possible by prayer. It's that simple, really.
>
> Through the people, the family and friends, that God put in my life, and their prayers, God spoke to me and said, "Will you love this boy who shot you?" And the best way that I could love him was to forgive him. Left to my own abilities, I don't think I would have done it. But it was through those around me, God speaking through them and touching me through them, that I was able to say yes. And I know that I would have died a long time ago had I not listened to God, said yes to God, followed the example of his Son, and loved and forgiven. . . .
>
> Everything that I've experienced in the last thirty-plus years can only be from God. At first I wondered why this was happening to me, to us, and a quiet, still voice – we all know what it is: God – spoke to me. After the shooting and throughout the hours, days, months, and years that have followed, that quiet, still voice has assured me that it's of God, from God, a blessing.

Catholics have their own criteria and process for sainthood. But as far as many a New Yorker is concerned, we can skip the formalities: McDonald is a saint for our times. He wasn't just a hero and role model. He allowed God to work powerfully through his suffering and weakness, and everyone whose life he touched came away blessed. ⤳

wish him a good morning, and how during his college years his father would make a weekly trip to Boston just to have lunch together at Applebee's. "My father was always committed to me. He did more than most able-bodied fathers could ever do with their sons. . . . My parents created the most phenomenal life out of such darkness. It was due to their unmatched, unconditional devotion and love for each other, which I witnessed from the beginning of my life."

The Teacher Who Never Spoke

MAUREEN SWINGER

How my brother who could never walk or talk coached dozens of his peers into manhood

THE SUMMER my brother Duane turned twenty, a formidable young man stayed with us on a break from the Ivy League. He had never, to anyone's knowledge, lost an argument. Several weeks into his visit, my mother walked into the dining room where my brother and his friend were, in theory, eating lunch. In reality, both men were sitting at the table with locked jaws. One didn't have to say, "I need you to eat." The other didn't need to say, "Hell, no." They both knew exactly what was going on: the Ivy Leaguer was losing an argument to my brother, who had never learned to speak.

Duane was born healthy, as far as anyone could tell, but when he was three months old he was attacked by his first grand-mal seizure, with countless more to follow. He was diagnosed with Lennox-Gastaut syndrome, a rare form of epilepsy, and his seizures were so brutal that the doctors didn't think he'd live out the year. That one year turned into thirty-one and a half.

Often when I tell people about my brother, I see questions in their faces: "Why was he ever born? Why put him through needless suffering? Why dedicate your family's time and energy to a hopeless case? Why spend all that money?" These questions reflect a worldview so widely accepted today that most people don't even realize they hold it: that of utilitarianism. Yet its principles are constantly invoked in debates over right or wrong, for instance in regard to abortion or physician-assisted suicide.

Most famously advanced by John Stuart Mill, utilitarianism argues that an action is good only because it maximizes a given benefit. This school of thought's most prominent champion today is the Australian philosopher Peter Singer, a professor of bioethics at Princeton University. In Singer's version of utilitarianism – which is in many ways just an especially forthright articulation of our culture's worldview – to act ethically means to seek to maximize the satisfaction of people's desires. This, in Singer's view, also means that we must seek to minimize the suffering of people unable to have or express preferences – if necessary, through terminating their lives before or after birth. People such as Duane.

Opposite, Federico Marcolla, Sacred Gaze

In 1980, the "save the children from existing" philosophy hadn't reached southwest Pennsylvania, where my parents lived. And before Duane's birth, they had no idea there was anything different about him. But if they had known, I know what my parents would have said: "He's our son."

Nobody knows how much Duane could understand. In one aptitude test, he showed no interest in differentiating a red square from a yellow triangle, and the neurologists told us that he had the cognition of a three-month-old. We were amused. How do you measure intelligence in someone so full of life, whose constant seizures played havoc with his memory and situational awareness? Snapshot neurological tests can't capture the reality of his life.

Can Singer or other utilitarians do any better than the neurologists? For many in this camp, not all members of the human species are considered persons. Personhood, they argue, requires self-awareness and the ability to conceive of future goals and plans: to experience oneself as having interests. Duane would not have qualified. In his case, utilitarianism would say that another good – reducing suffering – should have kicked in. No doubt Singer would allow that my parents' preference to keep Duane alive should have weight (after all, they are "persons," even if he supposedly wasn't). But still, by Singer's account, there was nothing in Duane himself that could have made it wrong to kill him.

Christians do not think like this. In Christian terms, an action is good not only because it has beneficial consequences, but because it is good in itself. What's more, good actions have the power to change for the better those who do them. We seek to love like God – to be merciful, honorable, and just – because we want to reflect his character: to "become like Christ,"

to grow into "the knowledge of the Son of God, to maturity, to the measure of the stature of the fullness of Christ," as Paul writes in his letter to the Ephesians. It is this *becoming* that guides our decisions, because all choices change us – in one direction or another.

Wheelchairs and Fireworks

But I can't leave these questions in the safe world of abstractions. I wish you could have known my brother.

To someone glancing toward him once, only to quickly look away, this was Duane: A lanky body in a high-support wheelchair, eyes often vacant, staring a hole in the ceiling. One of his wrists was noticeably contracted, and yes, he drooled.

But talk to anyone who spent time with him, and none of them will mention this. Because that wasn't essential to who he was. And part of my bone-deep conviction that Singer's arguments are wrong is my experience of Duane as a person. Whatever his level of intellectual development, he was *someone*. Someone who, even in Singer's terms, had interests, someone who had a good purpose for which he was made.

Who was this someone? He had an impish grin, a mischievous sideways glance from coffee-brown eyes that you only saw if you were at eye level – and if he wasn't in a post-seizure daze.

He derived enormous satisfaction from the little things that made up his day. You earned a huge smile just for shifting him to a more comfortable position. Kids fiddling with the knobs on his chair were enough to bring on the giggles. If he was watching fireworks, he would laugh till he choked. "Breathe, D, breathe!" we'd beg. Then, whoosh . . . BOOM! The next one lit the sky, and D was off again. And when he was mad the world knew that too. If he had tired of sitting around at church or at dinner, he'd let you know with a "get-me-out-of-here" roar.

The five of us siblings were born within the space of five years, with D right in the middle of the lineup. As kids we prayed confidently for miraculous healing, sure that the next morning he'd run out of his room to meet us. But sooner or later, the realization caught up with each of us: D is D, and he's here, as he is, for a reason.

That discovery didn't make life easier for our family. We can scan back over thirty-one years and celebrate the wondrous times. But slowing the frames, more lonely scenes come into view: the sleepless nights, the sprints to the hospital, the ache we sometimes felt of always being different.

To be sure, we were among the most supported of families caring for a child with special needs. As young people, my parents had joined the Bruderhof, a movement founded on Jesus' call to love one another. We lived in an intentional community of three hundred people committed to serving each other throughout life. Duane, in short, could not have landed anywhere better. And yet, even this did not supply his story with a tidy happily-ever-after.

While Duane was a young child, our family managed all of his home care. During the day the teachers at the Bruderhof's children's center included him in his peer group's activities. That worked, mostly, until he reached his teens. By then, he was taller than my dad, and if a seizure started during a transfer to or from his wheelchair, he could hurl himself and his care-giver to the ground. Starting in ninth grade, he spent his days off the community premises, at a school for children with special needs.

Our team of siblings had by now developed into a capable crew of nursing aides, cooks, and errand runners, all of us proud to "manage"

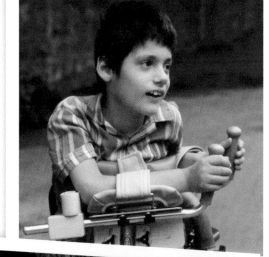

Duane at age five *(above)*; with the author *(middle)*; and with his parents, Jeremy and Mengia Bazeley *(bottom)*

looking after Duane. (My brother Evan was the first responder, with a knack for sleeping through Duane's deafening happy noises, but waking the moment he heard the muffled grunts of a grand-mal seizure starting.) Nobody but us witnessed the crazy nights, and we didn't talk about them. We hardly realized ourselves how worn down we were getting.

From the outside, it looked fine. Duane could go anywhere and be met with joyous greetings. People in the community cared about him. But not many truly knew him, or ever met *him* without a family member or aide at his side.

In retrospect, I see how much our family, all rather stubborn individualists, benefited from those often-strenuous years. Would we ever have become a team if we hadn't been tested? We discovered that love is action – often the same action over and over. We learned that prayer had better come before any action.

We also learned that encouraging words from others had their place, but that some expressions backfired. Take the word *gift*. People often told us what a gift Duane was. And yes, he was a gift, wrapped in incredibly complex packaging, a present that could tear your heart in two. But hearing the word, I was sometimes only just able to bite back a snarky "Would you like to do the night shift with our gift?"

In the end, this was the form of love that we learned to value: someone showing up to take Duane on a walk. Someone hosting a fireworks show for his birthday. Someone looking him in the eye and saying, "How's it going?" without worrying about getting an answer.

Becoming a Teacher

Then a new pastor arrived at the Bruderhof community where we lived in upstate New York. Richard Scott was funny, British, not too tall, and very perceptive. He looked Duane in the eye, and Duane looked back. Richard didn't only see a boy in a wheelchair who needed complex care. He saw a teacher without any students, a missionary without a mission field.

> # Nothing you've excelled at till now counts for much.

And he noticed something else: that other young men in the community, despite hearing about dedication and service all their lives, can easily hit their twenties without any significant testing – and perhaps without much motivation beyond sports, music, or self-serving career ambitions.

Richard wasn't only worried about these young men's futures but also about the community's present. If we weren't finding a place for Duane to help work for the kingdom among us, didn't that indicate a kind of blindness – an inability to see as Christ sees? These concerns came to an unexpected head at one community meeting in which we were reading together from an essay by Bruderhof founder Eberhard Arnold:

> Again and again, what it amounts to is a clash between two opposing goals: One goal is to seek the person of high position, the great person, the spiritual person, the clever person . . . the person who because of his natural talents represents a high peak, as it were, in the mountain range of humanity. The other goal is to seek the lowly people, the minorities, the disabled, the prisoners: the valleys of the lowly between the heights of the great. . . . The first goal aims to exalt the individual, by virtue of his natural gifts, to a state approaching the divine. In the end he is made a god. The other goal seeks the wonder and mystery of God becoming man, God seeking the lowest place among us.

At these words, my father cried out, leaped from his chair, and ran out of the room weeping. The rest of my family was frozen in place. After all, Arnold's words, though vivid, expressed a familiar idea, one we'd heard in church before. Perhaps we were a little too used to hearing it.

It is not that Christianity glorifies suffering for its own sake. Even Jesus suffered on the cross "for the sake of the joy that was set before him." It is not that Christian teaching denies that sickness should, and will, be healed. Rather, we are convinced that God is in the business of exalting the lowly, that he takes his place in the frailest of bodies, that his "power is made perfect in weakness."

My father heard that truth in Arnold's words that day. So did Richard. And in a community meeting not long afterward, he offered a startling proposal: what if Duane came home from his school for special needs – to teach? What if a new generation of young men became his students?

What happened next was nothing short of a revolution. The young men stepped up, and Duane's life took an astounding new turn.

The School of Duane

Are you ready to be Duane's student? Your crash course includes pushing his tricycle for hours, massaging his thin legs to relieve muscle cramps, and getting more oatmeal into his mouth than onto his shirt. It also includes finding that nothing you've excelled at till now counts for much here. Best tackle on the field? Meaningless. D needs help simply turning over in bed. Straight-A student? Who cares? D never even graduated from kindergarten. You're sociable, clever? Useless. Conversations are basically a one-way street.

The real kicker is standing by him through a seizure. You can do nothing to stop or ease it. All you can do is keep him clear of hard surfaces and stroke his shaking shoulder. Then he will fall asleep for hours, leaving you with another assignment – the lesson of quiet. Life is not always a party with continuous background noise and witticisms flying. There must also be hours when you weep for lost chances and lost people and lost time. In turn, those hours can give way to a silence in which you begin to hear God's hope for your life. Duane could take people there.

Duane shredded many of the rules we so often unwittingly live by: "Get ahead," "Don't commit yourself," "Watch your back." They all seem necessary – even as they drag us down under a burden of self-protection that leaves no room for costly obligations, or for love.

Dozens of young men now had the chance to change those rules.

So the household expanded, and two care-givers at a time came to live with us, rotating nights in D's room. Gaining a crew of adopted sons, my parents also rediscovered the benefits of an eight-hour night. My mom, a legend among alumni of the School of Duane for her five-star bakery, was continually startled at the speed at which her cinnamon rolls disappeared.

My parents prayed for each of these young men, knowing that they often came to Duane's door at a time when their own forward momentum had stalled. Some were not sure of their faith. Some were not sure of their future. Some were letting go of a love that wasn't meant to be, and some didn't yet know what love was.

What Duane taught varied from person to person. But nobody graduated from his school unchanged. After he died, my parents were inundated with letters. One man wrote,

> During my early twenties my life was fraught with struggle and confusion, till I got the chance to care for Duane. . . . He taught me that I really didn't know it all, that I had to start caring for others first . . . that perfection and strength as God sees them were utterly different from my previous strivings for those qualities. I don't know where I'd be without having known him.

Duane's care was physically and mentally demanding. You could never park him an inch too close to the table, or forget to set his brakes. Transfers from bed to chair required both gentleness and strength. Through it all, D was patient. Yes, he could holler when he had to, but he trusted you through everything that didn't go right.

Caring for him was also fatherhood training. Graduates of Duane's school could face whatever came along with humor, patience, and grace: basic nursing, daunting diapers, or a string of sleepless nights. They learned leadership, humility, and the necessity of prayer. Many future families were to benefit.

Gaining a Guardian

As my parents reached their sixties, my brother Brendan and his wife Miriam stepped up their support, becoming de facto house parents and Duane-team guides. Their kids sang Duane awake in the mornings and played catch with their teddy bears in his big, high-railed bed. My parents had always dreamed of visiting Europe, and now a small community in Germany invited them for an extended stay. They asked Brendan and Miriam to become Duane's legal guardians – "but," with a twinkle, "we are still his parents!"

Their travels were punctuated by phone calls, checking in with base camp. Brendan gave updates; Duane grinned at the familiar but insubstantial voices. Any changes in therapy or medication were discussed with the home team, the parents-on-tour, and the community's medical staff. It proved to be a stable triangle.

Duane had always had the best possible medical care. His doctors, who were members of our community, had known him since babyhood. They had seen Duane through several intensive surgeries for seizure management (with varying positive results; none was a magical cure). Through good, bad, and downright wretched days, they had loved him like a son. If Dr. Jonathan Zimmerman looked over some heads at a church service and didn't like Duane's color, he'd appear with his stethoscope afterwards, and he wouldn't leave till he had things figured out.

Still, when Duane turned thirty, no one would have guessed he was heading into his final year. He had outlived plenty of specialists' predictions. Meanwhile, though, his old friend Richard was dying of cancer. Perhaps his own impending mortality made Richard aware of something we couldn't yet see. One evening, he spoke to Brendan and Miriam with the directness of one who does not have many words left: "When Duane's time comes, let him go. You

L'Arche: A Two-Way Training Ground

Photography by Warren Pot and Tomasz Sewilski

L'Arche communities are made up of people with and without disabilities sharing life. At the heart of L'Arche is a belief in the sacredness and unique value of each person and a recognition that everyone can contribute.

Photography by Warren Pot and Tomasz Sewilski

and I know that he'll get the best medical care in the world. But don't try to stop him from going home."

Richard died on February 7, 2011. For Duane, there was one more summer full of his favorite things: chilling by the lake with burgers and a beer, quality time with old friends, fireworks. Alumni dropped in, now with families in tow, to introduce their kids to their teacher. But when his parents came home from their travels, they saw a change in his eyes.

By September, it was clear that Duane's body was beginning to wear out. After years of tireless care, his medical team had to face the fact that nothing further could be accomplished except in the way of pain relief. As our family talked through hard decisions, we knew: after more years with him than we thought we'd ever get, his time was coming to an end.

Through a cold autumn, he was mostly in bed. His visitors ranged from medical staff to the community's kindergarten class, always ready to break into raucous song. He had his enormous picture window and his favorite meals, when he wanted them. But he was partly elsewhere; when I spoke to him, he looked through me and then pulled back his gaze as if focusing on someone two feet away was difficult after peering into eternity.

He died so quietly that his brother Gareth, holding his hand, could hardly tell when he'd gone. But his eyes, which had been glazed and half-closed all day, were wide open and clear. He had not smiled in days; he was smiling. And it was a smile of surprised, joyous awe.

Just before his funeral, our family found ourselves standing shoulder to shoulder around him in the pattern we had adopted over the years: D as the hub, we as the spokes. We looked down at his still face in the pine casket, and marveled at his thirty-one intensely lived years.

Brendan read from *Adam, God's Beloved,* an account of Henri J. M. Nouwen's time caring for a young man with a condition similar to Duane's:

> While looking at Adam's quiet face, we prayed in gratitude for the gift of his years of life, and for all that he had brought to us in his great physical weakness and incredible spiritual strength. . . . Here is my counselor, my teacher, and my guide, who could never say a word to me, but taught me more than any book, professor, or spiritual director. He is dead now. His life is over. His task is accomplished. . . . I felt an immense sadness, but also an immense gladness. I'd lost a companion and gained a guardian for the rest of my life.

There were a handful of guys from the National Guard at the funeral. Those men, young, strong, and healthy, shoveled the earth into Duane's

These photos show some of the ways members take care of each other: cooking, shopping, creating art, dancing, and celebrating moments big and small together.

grave, saluting someone who could never stand on his own. I pictured Duane now, free from pain in his resurrected body, throwing his shoulders back, standing to his full six feet, and, free of the wheelchair, breaking into a joyous sprint.

The Upside-Down Truth

What was Jesus talking about when he said that the last will be first, and why does he accord such honor to "the least of these"? He calls them his brothers. He says that the door to his kingdom will open to the people who spend time with them, even if they are just offering a glass of water.

When he says "last" and "least," Jesus is talking the language of our present world, not of his kingdom; he is pointing out the position to which we relegate people we see as unimportant. But he also says that his kingdom is not an otherworldly domain of future happiness for good people. It's a real, boots-on-the-ground, right-now kingdom happening around us. What if "the least" are actually powerful commandos making inroads for their leader in enemy territory?

At Duane's graveside, in the November sunlight, our family stood surrounded by more than three hundred of his friends. From out of the crowd, Alan, born with Noonan Syndrome, marched up and stood between my parents. I could almost hear D saying, as he passed the torch to his younger comrade, "Go get 'em, tiger. Crack some more hearts open."

To crack a cold heart, to train it in love, is the most liberating service any person can do for another. These gifts do not show up on an ultrasound. They aren't mentioned in the first diagnosis of disability. They aren't measured by tests, and they aren't included in studies on compassionate euthanasia.

And that's why Duane's story is more than a tale of a great kid growing up in a caring family, and more than a testament to the abstract idea that all people's lives have value. There are people living bravely with disabilities everywhere. Many have strong networks of care, and many are devastatingly alone. Are the healthy individuals who pass them by, though, less alone? Perhaps it is isolation from humanity that breeds the sort of clinical coldness that suggests the removal of suffering by removing the one who suffers. Could the quest to eliminate others' suffering be a disguised attempt to distance *ourselves* from pain, because we fear there is no way through it?

My father heard a quote during a church service, and in that moment all the hurt stored up over the years erupted for everyone to see. Yet his love and care continued quietly

Many assistants come to L'Arche wanting to help those in need. They often are surprised to discover that the members with disabilities become *their* teachers and mentors, in matters of the heart and in becoming fully human.

through all the years to come, steadied by faith and humor. My mother wept at the graduations of Duane's classmates, and at their weddings. Yet while grieving deeply for what could never be, she completely embraced what was. Is it possible to protect ourselves from grief? What if we end up protecting ourselves from love?

To reach through this pain to the love beneath, we need resources beyond the imagination of utilitarians like Peter Singer. Yes, Duane "provided value" to many. Yes, our lives are richer because he was in them. But my parents, and the other members of the Bruderhof, were not waiting to see if this would be the case before they decided whether Duane was worthy of regard. He did not need to prove to anyone that he was an asset. It was the reverse: he was able to contribute because his community knew that he was valuable anyway, as a brother. His presence with us brought the image of God to light – within him *and* within those who cared for him.

> To crack a cold heart, to train it in love, is the most liberating service any person can do for another.

Duane's claim to be "someone who counts" didn't depend on his being (to use Singer's language) biographically aware of himself as having interests. His life, like all our lives, is sacred because he, like the rest of us, was drafted into this existence, into this peace-bringing army of the sons of Adam. Our duties are assigned, and we may not go absent without leave.

This wisdom is not in any ethics textbook. Those attempting to determine what is right or wrong for people like Duane ought to come live alongside – but only if they are ready to have some ethics applied in the reverse direction. That's how dozens of young men came to experience this truth, which the utilitarian project rejects as an outmoded relic. These students thank Duane – my brother and theirs – for an education that completely overturned their judgments of value and success. At the end of the line, they encountered the last; then the whole line turned, and the last was in the lead. ⤻

Maureen Swinger is an editor at Plough.

L'Arche was founded in 1964 by Canadian humanitarian Jean Vanier. There are now over 140 L'Arche communities in the world. For more information visit *larche.org.*

Harlem Postcards

I.

Palm Sunday
(Amsterdam Avenue at 142nd Street)

High noon, and an azure sky,
waving branches, a festive crowd;
the shimmer of heat and springtime silk.
(Tomorrow, of course, the forgotten fronds
will be swept together, bagged, and burned.
One day's enough for praise – and besides,
the city streets have to be kept clean.)

II.

Via Crucis
(Central Park West at 110th Street)

Good Friday, and the endless rain
is streaming down the wet black face
of the rocks that tower above the park.
Rain, and red-flecked crabapple petals:
tears from a thorn crown, dropping like blood.
Rain, drip-dropping in the echoing cave
of the crowded subway, where a man stands tall.
He's regal, despite the harried mob.
"Jesus is coming!" he cries with fervor.
"Jesus is coming! Are you ready?"

Easter Morning
(Morningside Avenue at 127th Street)

Here comes the sun, to light the alleys,
to flood each lonely garret and caress each stiffened limb.
Here comes the sun, to search out the dejected,
to warm the huddled drunk and make the panhandler sing.
Here comes the Son, to satisfy the hungry,
to mend the broken spirit, and lift the gravest sin.

CHRISTOPHER ZIMMERMAN

PHOTOGRAPHY BY DAVE BECKERMAN

Bonhoeffer in China

An Interview with Dissident Writer Yu Jie

PETER MOMMSEN

Above and following three spreads, Wu Guanzhong, *The Yangtze River in 1974, oil, 20 x 603 cm*

Plough: You've been described as "one of China's most prominent essayists and critics" (*New York Review of Books*). Yet your books are now blacklisted in China, and you've been living in the United States since 2012. What made you seek political asylum abroad?

Yu Jie: On October 8, 2010, it was announced that Liu Xiaobo, the Chinese dissident writer, had been chosen to receive the Nobel Peace Prize. At the time, he was in prison serving an eleven-year sentence for inciting subversion (he remains a prisoner today). The authorities knew that Liu and I were good friends – we had known each other for twelve years and I was writing his biography. Immediately after the announcement, my wife Liu Min and I were placed under house arrest.

The ceremony to award the Nobel Peace Prize to Liu in absentia was on December 10. The day before this was the darkest of my life. Plainclothes agents of the secret police kidnapped me from my home, pulled a black hood over my head, and brought me to a detention room. For six hours they tortured me almost to death. They told me: "If our supervisor gives the order, we will dig a hole and bury you alive." I was stripped of all my clothes and beaten badly as they took pictures. Then they forced my fingers backward one by one, saying that they would break the fingers I had used to write against the Communist Party. Eventually I lost consciousness.

The first hospital they brought me to refused to treat me. So they brought me to a more advanced hospital, where physicians told me that if the torture had continued another half hour I would not have survived.

Do you remember what you were thinking during the interrogation?

Before I lost consciousness I prayed to God in my heart. I clearly sensed his presence and felt the assurance: without the permission of God, not one hair of my head will fall. These words came to me as well: "Do not fear those who can kill the body, because they cannot kill the soul." Those two promises of Jesus were my prayer.

After my kidnapping, my wife was still under house arrest. All phone lines and the

Yu Jie and his family shortly after their arrival in the United States in January 2012

一九七四年長江 吳冠中 中志 于二00四年.

internet were cut off, and for five days she had no way of finding out where I was. She was under such stress that she lost half her hair. Fortunately, by divine providence, we had sent our two-year-old son for a visit to his grandparents shortly before, so he was spared this experience.

After my arrest and torture, they tried to bribe me – they promised that if I would stop criticizing the regime they would provide a platform for me to write popular literature, and I would get rich.

Even after my release, the harassment and periods of house arrest continued. I could not go to church or attend Bible study; I was cut off from my Christian brothers and sisters. I looked in my son's eyes and asked myself what kind of father I could be to him if we remained in China in this impossible situation. And so in January 2012 we came to the United States.

Awakening

You weren't raised as a Christian. Were there influences in your childhood and youth that laid the groundwork for your conversion later?

I was born in the city of Chengdu in the province of Sichuan, a beautiful, mountainous region with a long history of resisting the imperial power in Beijing. So from the beginning of my life I drank in a dislike for centralized power.

My father is an engineer. His thinking and lifestyle were quite westernized, and even as a young boy he treated me as an equal. In a Confucian culture that emphasizes hierarchy, this was rare.

The moment of my political awakening came when I was sixteen and attending high school. I still remember hearing the news of the mass murder of students protesting on Beijing's Tiananmen Square. That day, June 4, 1989, marked a turning point for me – I began to realize the true nature of the Communist regime. I would never believe their lies again.

Three years later, I arrived in Beijing myself, as a student at Peking University, China's oldest and most selective institute of higher learning. I studied there for eight years, earning a master's degree. But far more important to me than my formal coursework were my independent studies in the library. Thanks to a friendly librarian who bent the rules, I had access to restricted books published in Taiwan. I read accounts of the campaign of civil disobedience against Taiwan's authoritarian government in the 1970s and 80s, and learned how a pro-democracy movement can be successful. What especially impressed me was the prominent role that Taiwan's churches played in this movement.

But you were still just a secular observer.

That's right. In 1998, while still a graduate student, I published my first book, *Fire and Ice,* a collection of satirical essays criticizing Chinese society. Looking back, it amazes me that the book ever made it past the censors. But that was the year Bill Clinton visited China – the first US president to do so since the Tiananmen Square massacre. The Chinese leadership wanted Western media to portray China as a free society. What better way than to allow publication of a book critical of the regime?

Though the authorities' motives were cynical, my book benefited, and I gained one of my best friends: a copy reached Liu Xiaobo in prison. Two years later, he was released and we got to know each other. He introduced me to the Tiananmen Mothers, whose sons and daughters had died in Tiananmen Square. As a result, I became involved in the movement for human rights in China.

That year, 2000, I finished graduate school and Liu Min and I were married. We spent our first year together in the southeastern province of Guangdong, editing a pro-democracy textbook for schoolchildren – we wanted an alternative to the propaganda in government textbooks. One of our collaborators, a Christian, suggested including readings from the Bible, since it is a historically important text. His proposal was controversial, but my wife and I were intrigued. When we moved back to Beijing she began reading the Bible on the subway to and from work. Over time, what she read convinced her, and she became a Christian.

> **Our wish is to overcome the separation based on class and social status.**

It took me two years to follow her. One reason was the high status that traditional Chinese culture gives to scholars. Despite the Communist Party's official hostility to Confucianism, in reality we Chinese are still born and bred into a Confucian worldview. This has very positive aspects: we are educated to put the good of the whole nation – in fact, the whole world – above selfish goals. Yet Confucianism also strongly emphasizes self-cultivation: one strives to become a saint through one's own moral effort. To move from this way of thinking to Christianity's teaching of the total depravity of human nature – of course Calvinism is especially strong on this – was a huge shift for me.

Without the illumination of the Holy Spirit, I believe that people like me could never be humbled. As Chinese intellectuals, we feel we need to keep our dignity and face. Before my baptism, I remember telling my wife that I could never be baptized because the ceremony involved bowing to the minister.

The Beijing Ark

So given your reluctance, how did your baptism come about?

I was in a small room with about one hundred people in an underground house church. The pastor called my name and the Spirit came. I saw my depravity, my sinfulness, and the tears started flowing.

We then started a Bible study group of three couples. More and more people came, and we rented an apartment for our gatherings. Soon God sent a pastor to lead the church, which we wanted to be open to the public, not just a private fellowship. We didn't want to become a megachurch; our vision was to remain a small community in which we could know and love each other. We called it the Beijing Ark.

Many politically "sensitive" people joined our church: dissident writers, relatives of victims of Tiananmen Square, and lawyers who resisted the regime. Usually, people with such backgrounds have trouble finding a church

that will accept them – churches fear the secret police. Because we welcomed such people, we faced harassment. For example, in 2006, within two months we were forced to change our gathering place six times because the police pressured the landlords.

But our church isn't just made up of intellectuals. Migrants from the countryside also joined us, as did others with vocational jobs. One brother, who is now studying for the ministry, had formerly gotten rich through pirating translations of Harry Potter books – after converting, his life was transformed. All the members enjoy an intimate fellowship and relationship with one another; our wish is to overcome the separation based on class and social status.

That is why I will never leave the church community in which I was baptized and became a Christian. Even though I've now lived in the United States for five years, I am still a member of that church and stay in touch with the brothers and sisters.

By contrast, most Chinese intellectuals who convert and are baptized do not join a local church. They are scared of losing their independence and submitting to community life, partly because communism's form of community has brought so much fear and hurt. Even those who do attend church often avoid opening themselves to intimacy with brothers and sisters.

Now, I'm not claiming to be a better Christian than they are. But I do give thanks to God for calling me to a specific church community to which my wife and I can remain faithful.

My church helps me live my Christianity in real life – it's not just an abstract theory. For example, after my wife and I were put under house arrest, none of my Peking University friends and colleagues visited me. But many members of our church did. They had never read my books or engaged with my ideas – they are working people who have to put in long hours – but because we have the same Lord they came to visit us. They could not even enter our house; they had to stand outside the window and sing songs and give verbal greetings.

Christian Politics

What effect did your conversion have on your political activism?

Some people back away from activism after they become Christians, but my conversion made me even more convinced and enthusiastic to promote human rights. In my understanding, human rights are a gift from God, who created us and gave us life, liberty, and dignity. These rights are not determined by any national government. The Chinese government defines human rights as a right to survival – leaving humans little different than animals.

Religious freedom goes together intimately with other human rights; it is part of our comprehensive concern. We cannot isolate religious freedom, and it goes beyond just being free to worship God in a church building. Religious freedom includes freedom of the press, and the natural, God-given right of parents to educate their children according to their own beliefs.

Are there any ways your faith changed the way you approach politics?

Yes, it transformed my attitude quite radically. Before my conversion, I identified as a public intellectual, a scholar who functions as the conscience of society. I believed that since communism was responsible for so many evils and disasters, my responsibility was to help overthrow it. I put all my efforts into exposing the Communist Party's lies and publicizing its scandals.

After my conversion, I realized I was also a sinner. The problem isn't only the Communist Party – we all contribute to our world's evils. Now my focus is to think prophetically about how we can rebuild the nation after the collapse of communism. This rebuilding will happen through the transformation of human hearts by the message of Christ.

Since my transformation from humanist intellectual to Christian writer, I have gained more enemies. The Confucianists are against me because they see me as hostile to traditional Chinese culture. The nationalists are against me because I promote the universal kingdom of God.

> **If you attend a church that's being persecuted, you do so only for the sake of truth.**

Community and Resistance

You've written about the impact of Dietrich Bonhoeffer on you, especially his book *Life Together*. Why this book?

Life Together is enormously significant for Chinese Christian intellectuals, because so many of them treat Christianity individualistically, as a private matter, and never join in church life. When they talk about the Christian faith, they use a lot of philosophical terminology that excludes those with less education. One respected scholar who translated many Christian books into Chinese isolated himself in this way, and ended up becoming a fascist. So the common life with brothers and sisters is vital for our Christian discipleship. Bonhoeffer realized this. Even in the harshest of times he did his best to share some kind of communal life with others.

But Bonhoeffer also never saw community life as a form of withdrawal.

That's why he is one of the most important theologians for the Chinese church today. Our situation has certain analogies to that of German Christians under National Socialism – particularly since Xi Jinping took power as China's president four years ago. The church in China largely lacks the spiritual resources needed to face what is a critical moment for our whole society. The older churches tend to be fundamentalist and focused only on spiritual issues – they have little concern for what happens in the public square. Meanwhile, the newer churches emerging in the cities lack a robust connection to the great traditions of Christianity, including the Reformers. They are most influenced by popular American church culture: extremely charismatic worship, the prosperity gospel, and a megachurch model based on numbers. In Beijing and Shanghai, there are even churches whose membership is restricted to wealthy businesspeople.

Lacking roots, these new churches too often fall into a dangerous trap: they acculturate rather than resist. In this sense, I see them as reenacting what happened to the Chinese Protestants who chose to cooperate with the Communists in Chairman Mao's day by joining the government-controlled church known as the Three-Self Patriotic Movement. This church, which still exists, originated as a political manipulation by the Communist Party during the Korean War that sought to merge Christians into the pro-regime patriotic movement. By acceding, the church surrendered its particular truth and independent voice. Now we're seeing something similar with the new prosperity-gospel churches, which compromise on matters of principle and conscience in order to stay in the regime's good graces.

In such circumstances, the testimony of Bonhoeffer is extremely important – not only his ideas, but even more his example of giving his life for the faith. Bonhoeffer personally participated in the anti-Hitler movement. His witness should provoke us to think about how to unite Christian faith with resistance.

Because of Persecution

Tertullian said, "The blood of the martyrs is the seed of the church." Is that true of the church in China?

Based on our experiences in the Beijing Ark, absolutely, because persecution has purged the church. If you attend a church that's being persecuted, you do so only for the sake of truth – you cannot have other motives. From the Bible and church history we see that true believers in every age go through persecution of some kind. We have an Asian proverb: "Causes for worry stimulate life, but pleasure and ease bring on death."

Because of the persecution of our church community, our bond of brotherhood is really strong. Take, for example, the brother in my church who was shot in the leg in Tiananmen; because he is crippled, it takes him half an hour longer to get to church, and yet he is always punctual. Churches here in America enjoy more freedom, yet many arrive late for worship or play with their smartphones during the service. And because of the relatively opulent lifestyles of the congregants, many pastors are careful not to offend. Their main concern is not the kingdom of God, but retaining members. In their sermons, I hear talk about grace, love, peace, and prosperity – but never a mention of sin, the law of God, or church discipline. This is what Bonhoeffer called "cheap grace."

In 2015, in the city of Wenzhou, the authorities forcibly removed crosses from the exterior of church buildings. What significance, if any, does this have for Christians elsewhere in China?

The aim is to destroy all prominent symbols of Christianity in the public sphere. What's happened in Wenzhou is a preview of what could happen across China under President Xi Jinping. Wenzhou is a large city in Zhejiang, a fertile province where Christianity has developed and increased quickly and where Xi Jinping used to be the provincial leader. This policy of persecution is not accidental – it is being implemented with the president's

knowledge, perhaps as a trial balloon for a policy that will later be rolled out nationally. If they succeed in crushing the churches in Wenzhou, they can easily do the same elsewhere.

> **We need a life together in small communities where people really care for one another.**

What astonishes me is that they are persecuting not just underground house churches but also the government-approved Three-Self Church. In early January, Gu Yuese, senior pastor of the most prominent Three-Self church in Zhejiang and vice-president of the denomination nationally, was arrested after a sermon in which he protested the destruction of crosses. (Of course, this wasn't the official charge – he was accused of embezzling.)

Although media interest has flagged, cross demolitions are still continuing in Zhejiang. Some Christians have resisted using civil disobedience – we should pray for them! But the majority of churches capitulated.

Did you find that surprising?

Unfortunately, no. Too many churches in Wenzhou were built up with a business-model approach. They sought to attract wealthy businesspeople – never mind if they sold fake products or bribed officials. This attitude infected the churches themselves. Why was there a church-building boom in Wenzhou? Because the congregations that had money bribed local officials and invested millions of dollars in new buildings. Perhaps it would have been better to spend the money on education, publishing, or other ways to build up the Christian community.

As a matter of fact, I actually don't view the cross on the church building as so important in itself. Even if the authorities remove the physical cross and demolish the church building, the cross of Christ is still in our hearts – nobody can remove and demolish that. What is happening may serve as a healthy reminder: Why invest millions of dollars in building big churches? Why not use the money for discipleship, theological training, and charity?

You've written that by 2030, China is projected to have the biggest Christian population of any country. What do you think will be the future of the church in China?

Firstly, numbers aren't what is most important. To my fellow Christians, I emphasize again and again: Christian life is not just Sunday worship. Our faith must impact our political life and all aspects of personal and social life. Unfortunately, too many Christians in China are still just Sunday Christians. Their faith is separated from their daily life.

Take the example of nationalism. When the government puts on nationalistic ceremonies featuring grand displays of military equipment, many Christians flock to these events enthusiastically. If you mention Taiwan's independence, they will respond, "If Taiwan tries to assert its independence, we must attack them." They are indoctrinated just like the unbelievers. Similarly, too few Han Chinese Christians feel any sympathy for ethnic groups who are being oppressed, such as the Tibetans and Uighurs. They are Han Chinese nationalists first, and Christians second.

Christian Communism?

How do you suggest addressing this problem? Can the spiritual roots of the church in China be a resource for Chinese Christians today?

There is definitely a strong continuum from Chinese Christianity before communism. The remnants went underground, but the writings and legacy of Watchman Nee and others are still a great heritage and encouragement for us today. We have two groups to look to: the many foreign missionaries who gave their lives in the mission field, and also the many native pastors and church leaders who really loved the Lord and died for the truth.

Even if you might not find spiritual giants like Martin Luther or Bonhoeffer, by the grace of God we also have our saints, such as Watchman Nee and Wang Mingdao. Liao Yiwu, who wrote the book *God Is Red,* profiles others, such as Wang Zhiming, the pastor martyred in 1973 who is commemorated with a statue in Westminster Abbey. They are also to be found among public intellectuals, such as Sister Lin Zhao, a Peking University graduate who called the rule of Chairman Mao idol worship and demon possession. As a result, she was arrested and executed.

I think we need to go back further, to the model of the early church. We need a life together in small communities where people really know each other and care for one another.

That's the model of common life described in Acts 2 and 4. And of course, Bonhoeffer's call for community in *Life Together* draws on the same early Christian vision. What comparison or contrast would you draw between political communism and the community experienced in the first church in Jerusalem?

To my understanding, Karl Marx stole some ideas from the Bible and tried to realize that ideal community life through evil means, and that deformed the ideal. The biggest difference is that Karl Marx wanted to build a kingdom of heaven on earth by human power, and was willing to accept all kinds of means, such as revolution or mass killings of those who didn't agree with his ideas. In the Bible Jesus says, "My kingdom is not of this world." But the church is really somehow a reflection of the kingdom of God on earth.

As you look to the future, what are the things that give you hope?

First of all, I think our future, both in China and in America, is in the hand of our God. So that is my heart's comfort. That does not mean we are inactive. We do have a calling. We do have a mission to participate in his plan and to obey his will.

Through all this life experience and struggle, I have gained a clearer vision about God's plan for me. When the secret police came for me they had to confess, "Your pen is more dangerous than an army." So I don't despise my calling. ⤳

This article combines interviews conducted by Peter Mommsen on September 11, 2016, and January 12, 2017, with assistance from Leonard and Havilah King. Translation by Zhiyong Wang.

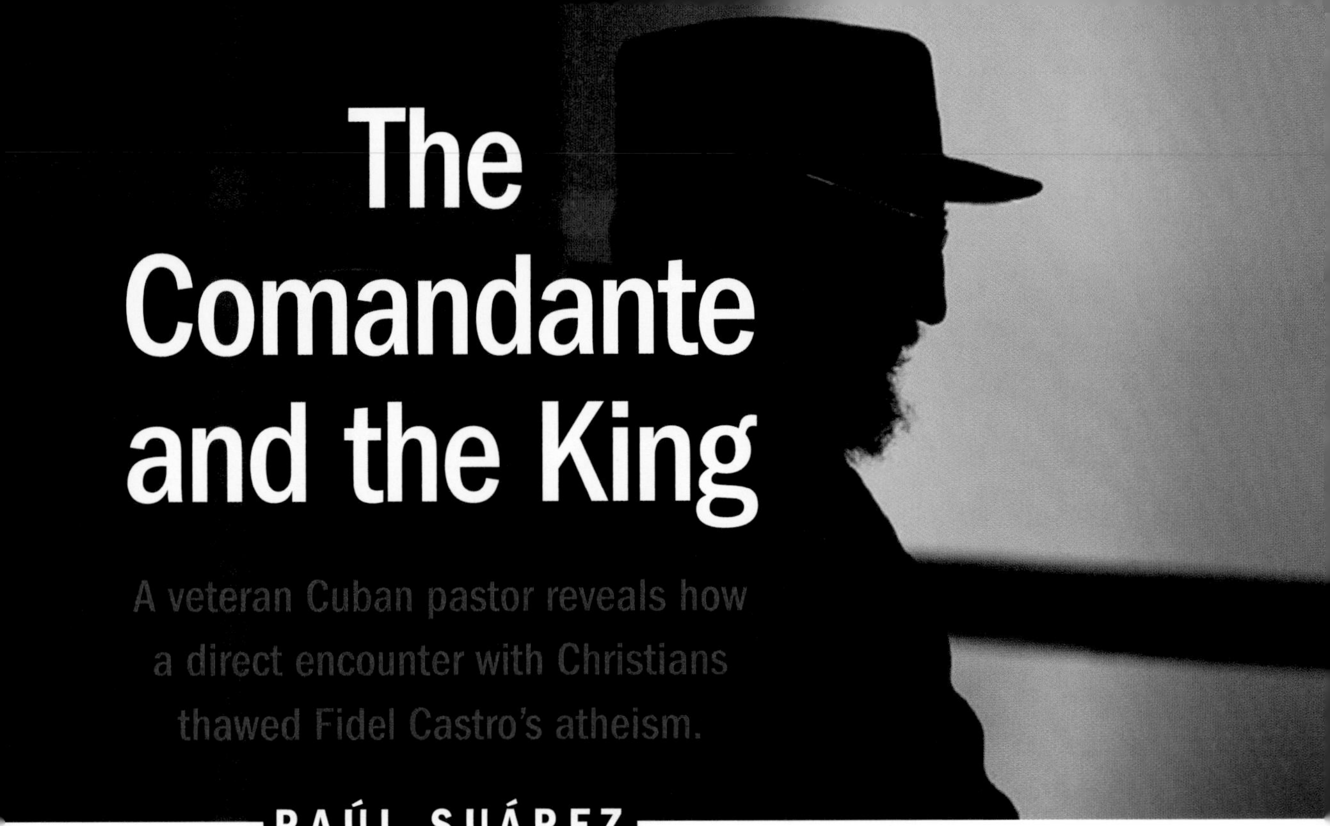

The Comandante and the King

A veteran Cuban pastor reveals how a direct encounter with Christians thawed Fidel Castro's atheism.

RAÚL SUÁREZ

AS TOLD TO SUSAN ARNOLD

DURING THE FIFTY-EIGHT YEARS since the Cuban Revolution brought communism to my country, Jesus' kingdom has been advancing in Cuba. As pastor of a Cuban church throughout these sometimes-difficult decades, I should know. Let me tell you my story.

I was born in a village on the northern coast of Cuba, where the sugarcane industry overshadowed every aspect of life. My father was a sugarcane cutter, which meant he worked at most three or four months a year. Life was hard. How do you feed a family of twelve when there is no work? When my siblings and I reached second or third grade, my father took us out of school. The girls cleaned, cooked, or washed for the landowners. They were paid next to nothing. We boys went to work in the fields, helping our father but earning nothing ourselves. Poverty and misery marked all of our lives, but together we survived. My father drank a lot, and his example prompted most of us to evade reality through alcohol.

I was sent to help a family in the country when I was eleven. After three years, I returned to town looking for work, which I found selling vegetables from a wheelbarrow. I was filled with hate and sadness, which I desperately tried to drown by drinking. One evening in December 1952, disgusted with the life I was living, I went to bed crying. I had no idea how to pray, but almost drowning in tears I repeated a Bible verse I had once learned, "Create in me a clean heart, O God, and renew a steadfast spirit within me." Immediately I felt something new, although I didn't understand what it was. That was the moment Jesus Christ came into my life. For the first time I could remember, I slept peacefully without being drunk.

Raúl Suárez is a Baptist pastor, founder and former director of the Martin Luther King Center in Havana, and a member of Cuba's National Assembly.

I began to attend church services and was baptized five months later. A visiting preacher challenged us to use the new life God had given us. I said I wanted to become a pastor. Although I was almost completely illiterate, I passed the entrance exam to enter seminary at seventeen, with the help of the preacher and his wife.

Becoming a Christian in a Changing Cuba

The seminary was sponsored by Southern Baptists, so almost all my professors were from the United States. Through their influence, I began to adopt a new outlook. I wasn't interested in what was happening in Cuban society, politics, and economics because the professors weren't interested. Then in January 1959, while I was still in seminary, Fidel Castro's revolutionary forces ousted US-backed dictator Fulgencio Batista. That was something one couldn't ignore. I became interested in what the new government was doing to benefit the poorest and most disadvantaged.

My wife Clara and I served as pastors in Colón for nine years. I was not of age for military service, but while we were there, I was drafted to the Military Units to Aid Production (UMAP). Despite its name, this wasn't really military service, but rather a system of forced agricultural labor camps for Christians, criminals, conscientious objectors to military service, homosexual men, and anyone else the revolutionaries labeled perverse. That experience taught me that even though I had no pulpit or church, I did not cease to be a Christian pastor. In 1968, the government ended the UMAP system, and I returned home to Clara, my son Joel, and my newborn daughter Raquel.

Although many Christians fled the country, Clara and I saw that the revolution did accomplish many good things. We couldn't condemn it wholesale and flee; we had to find ways to address the bad things we saw. The life of a

> **The life of a Christian extends beyond the four walls of the church.**

Above,
Raúl Suárez
in his church
in Havana

Left,
Fidel Castro with Jesse Jackson and Raúl Suárez, June 1984

Right,
Suárez and Castro at a meeting with Cuban church leaders

Christian extends beyond the four walls of the church. If we want things to change, we have to get involved where the problems are and work at them, without being Communists, without being politicians, but by being Christians. At this time, I read the Bible in a new light. The Bible tells us we are to be the salt of the earth, the light of the world, the yeast that makes the dough rise. Yeast makes bread soft – if you don't put yeast in, it will be hard as rock. When Christ tells us to be yeast, he wants us to be an element of transformation in society.

"Comandante, Take Off Your Hat"

In 1971, I became pastor of Ebenezer Baptist Church in Havana. At the time, scientific atheism was the official position of the Cuban government; Christians were viewed as second-class citizens and barred from government service and certain professions, including education. It was also difficult for a Christian to get a better job, and church activities were severely restricted.

In June 1984, Fidel Castro invited Rev. Jesse Jackson, a US presidential candidate, to visit Cuba. Jackson didn't want to be invited only by the government but also by a Cuban church, so we invited him through the Cuban Ecumenical Council. Fidel – in Cuba, he's universally known by his first name – asked Jackson to speak at the University of Havana. From there,

the whole group, including Fidel, came to the door of our church.

We were having a service that day. We thought Fidel would just drop them off and go. What a surprise we had when one of his bodyguards said, "Comandante, take off your hat, you are entering a church!" He took off his hat, came in, put his hand on my shoulder, and said, "Look, I don't know anything about your church; I only know the Catholic Church. Sit by me so when I have to do something, I can ask you and you can tell me what to do." I told him, "That's fine, you just do what I do."

Later in the service, a young Christian from Jackson's group asked Fidel to say a few words. He asked me, "What should I do?" I told him, "You don't have to preach, just greet everyone." So he spoke for five minutes. The whole thing was broadcast on television, and while Fidel was talking he had a Bible open on the pulpit in front of him and a cross behind him.

I wrote Fidel a letter thanking him for the visit and asking to meet with him. As far as I know, that was the first time anyone from the churches met with him. The Cuban Ecumenical Council wrote a document outlining our complaints. We discussed these with Fidel, and at the end he said, "I know some of you don't drink, but I want to make a toast. It's not too strong." (It was daiquiris.) "If any of you are teetotalers, just wet your lips." His toast was to make an agreement: "From now on, you work with the churches to understand what we are doing to help people, and I will work with my people to understand you." When he said that, everyone took a drink; it was like saying amen!

There were changes after that. The government eliminated certain provisions in the constitution and added new ones guaranteeing religious liberty, not only for us but for all religious groups. Before that time hardly any Bibles came into Cuba. Today, between one and two hundred thousand Bibles come into Cuba every year.

Doing God's Work in a Communist Country

In 1990, Fidel Castro went to the inauguration of the Brazilian president. When he arrived in Brazil, he was invited to visit some Christians. "If there were Christians like you in Cuba," he told them, "they could even have Party membership." That was printed in the papers. Clara and I didn't like that – as if in Cuba there weren't already Christians doing good things. So we wrote Fidel a letter. When he returned from Brazil, he called me up and said, "Get twenty Christians together, and we'll talk about that letter you wrote me."

At the meeting, we read Bible passages to Fidel and sang hymns. Afterward the Party changed its statutes and removed atheism as a requirement for membership. Finally believers who wished could become members of the Party. Although I have never been a member of the Party, there are many in the church who are. At the same time, the constitution was amended to remove the provisions promoting an atheist state and to specify the right of all citizens to hold religious beliefs and to practice the religion of their preference.

Around that time, too, a new electoral law was enacted. The Cuban Workers Union from the local neighborhood asked me if I would serve as their candidate to the National Assembly. I asked for time to decide. I spoke with my family, the church, and my neighbors. Finally I responded that if they would accept me as a pastor, I would accept. There was no problem. I won 94 percent of the vote in my district. From that time on I have been a member of the Assembly.

I do not earn a cent for this work. I am there because I am a pastor and a Christian, and because I am not afraid to work with people who think differently from me. I have never left an Assembly session feeling I needed to ask God for forgiveness for what I had said or for being there. I ask forgiveness for other things, but whenever I talk in the Assembly, I pray before I speak (and I speak in almost every meeting). I have often defended Christ's cause in the Assembly. There are Christians who don't understand or don't agree with my decision. But a person first has to be in agreement with his own heart and his own conscience. And that has allowed me to get this far as a Christian and has given me the courage to continue in the Assembly.

> True prosperity is the abundant life in Jesus.

What Role Will the Church Play in Cuba's Future?

When President Obama came to Cuba in 2014, he gave a speech trying to sell capitalism to the Cubans. But Cuba has not renounced socialism. Most Cubans have no intention of leaving the original ideals of the revolution, which are to build a new society on community values. Raúl Castro says, "The people elected me not to destroy socialism, but to save it." Now, we asked ourselves, what kind of socialism is Raúl Castro talking about? He defines it as prosperous socialism, prosperous in the sense that the needs of the people should be satisfied. People should earn more so that they can live better.

When Raúl Castro said that, we in the church discussed what the Bible teaches about prosperity. And there we discovered that true prosperity is the abundant life in Jesus Christ. People should have a good quality of life both spiritually and materially. People should be able to earn enough with work and creativity to support a family. In our churches there should be no needy people. A church where some people can bathe every day and have nice clothes and good food while in the same church others cannot survive the winter because they have nothing to keep them warm and little food – this is not God's will.

Right now many old people in Cuba are suffering; the church needs to get involved to see how to make this better. Another essential task of the church is to educate our children. We must teach them from a Christian point of view so they accept the good news of Christ, which is complete liberation – not just the freedom that comes from forgiveness of sins, but also a change of mentality that rejects selfishness and unites people. Singing hymns, reading the Bible, prayer, and preaching are all good, but the goal is to form community values, unselfish values.

Fidel Castro's death on November 25, 2016, affected the Cuban people deeply. Although he has been demonized abroad, the social changes he masterminded have allowed our people to reach a standard of living we never had in the past, and he will continue to be an inspiration as we meet the challenges of the immediate future. Thanks to all we've been through since the revolution, an ethical, moral, spiritual thread runs through Cuban culture, influencing the social and political life of the people. Those of us who still believe in this project of creating a more just and more human society will continue to care for this legacy.

After all, Fidel Castro didn't invent these ideals. They have been integral to Christianity from its very beginning. The Bible gives a clear

The Sermon on the Mount is the model we must follow to create scattered but united communities.

picture of how the early Christian communities "had everything in common" and distributed their goods "to all, as any had need" (Acts 2:44–45). Eberhard Arnold, who founded the Bruderhof community movement in 1920, was convinced that it is still possible to build such communities, where members are "of one heart and one soul." By living and sharing together, no one should be in need.

This vision brought Arnold to believe that private property is at the root of many of the evils in modern society. From the beginning, his pastoral vision was to build a productive, sustainable community that would be actual good news to the dispossessed and oppressed, the widows and orphans, the foreigners and slaves. Just as Peter's sermon at Pentecost called out a "faithless and perverse generation," such a community, if authentic, would be a prophetic fellowship. It would, by its sheer existence, repudiate the powers of sin, inequality, and injustice in a class society.

I have printed and distributed a Spanish edition of Arnold's *God's Revolution: Justice, Community, and the Coming Kingdom* to churches throughout Cuba. In this book, Arnold recaptures the importance of Jesus' prayer, "Thy kingdom come, thy will be done, *on earth* as it is in heaven," and of his words to his disciples that "the kingdom of God is in the midst of you" (Luke 17:21). But Arnold also makes another very important point, which the Cuban church and followers of Christ everywhere should never forget: the kingdom of God can neither be reduced to, nor fulfilled in, any political, economic, or social system.

Havana,
Cuba, 2017

As the early Christians taught, we must both see and be "seeds of the Word," signs of the kingdom that sprout throughout history, even if that kingdom's fullness awaits us in God's future. We are called to work with "hunger and thirst for justice" toward that great day here and now.

As we seek a new economic model in Cuba, the history of this communal movement, the Bruderhof, is an incentive to be faithful and above all to hold on to communal values so that there is no space, however small, for consumerism, individualism, profiteering, or the destruction of God's creation. Without a doubt, these are the causes that have led humanity to the brink of ethical, moral, and spiritual catastrophe, putting life on our planet at risk.

Finally, in these times when the victory of evil over good, death over life, the letter of the law over the spirit of the law, otherworldliness over the integrity of creation seems a fact, we must return to the source, Jesus of Nazareth. We must reconsider the church structure that has taken shape since the time of Constantine, an imperial church and a Christian empire lacking the essence of the communities founded by Jesus. The Sermon on the Mount is the model we must follow to create scattered but united communities – to continue to build, wherever we live, church community as a visible sign of the beloved community that awaits us in God's future. In this task, as Martin Luther King Jr. says, "the arc of the moral universe" is on our side. ⤳

Translated by Susan Arnold. This article is based on interviews on June 1–7, 2016, and January 4, 2017.

Confronted by Dorothy

A Christian Activist Reckons with a Modern-Day Saint

D. L. MAYFIELD

Opposite, Dorothy Day in the Catholic Worker office, 1965

I picked up a button about a decade ago with a quote attributed to Dorothy Day on it: "If you have two coats, you have stolen one from the poor." I loved this saying, loved the strength of conviction, the easy black-and-white application. I read more about Dorothy and became smitten. Her severe face and warm hands and intense sound bites were so soothing to my soul as I first read of her life and work and the Catholic Worker movement she helped start. I affixed that button to the front of my one orange-plaid corduroy coat and tromped around my neighborhood during the cold, gray Portland winters, hoping others would read it and be changed. If I am honest, a part of me wanted others to know how radical I was, how I had eschewed the things of the world, how hard I was trying to follow Jesus.

Now, years later, I have three coats: the orange-plaid corduroy still (even though the pockets have ripped), a raincoat (since I live in Oregon), and a longer, warm coat I bought for the three winters I spent in the Midwest. My Dorothy Day button now lives in a junk drawer, because I can't bear to wear it if it isn't true. Should I give one of my coats away? To whom should I give it? I live and work in a refugee and immigrant community; there are dozens of people I know who could use a coat. How do I pick? How do I navigate the enormity of the needs of the world, and my own response to them? I still don't know. And yet, even as I think these thoughts and feel like a failed radical, the words and life of Dorothy Day mean more to me than ever.

I take some comfort in knowing that Dorothy struggled with these same questions and contradictions throughout her life. Her feelings, I suspect, were complicated, since she was a unique and complex woman. She was driven, proud, dogmatic. She lived with fierce conviction in solidarity with the poor. She was also unsure, doubtful, and depressed from time to time due to the enormity of the suffering surrounding her. From a young age, Dorothy showed evidence of both her passion for justice and her quick mind. She was an activist, a sharp student, a curator of deep conversations. Her biographer, Robert Coles, noted that she was quick to dismiss her early life, preferring to talk instead of her conversion to Catholicism and how she met Peter Maurin, with whom she cofounded the Catholic Worker's newspaper and houses of hospitality. But the threads of her personality, strong convictions, and engaging writing style were already all there, and her years of struggle and wandering no doubt contributed to her profound empathy for those who suffer.

In her writings you can find diverging thoughts – she writes of always hiding her sadness, and also of the importance of feeling

---

D. L. Mayfield works with refugee communities and is author of Assimilate or Go Home: Notes from a Failed Missionary on Rediscovering Faith *(HarperOne, 2016). She lives in Portland, Oregon, with her husband and two children. This article is taken from her foreword to a new collection of Dorothy Day's writings,* The Reckless Way of Love *(see page 48).*

the full force of emotions. These contradictions reassure me, reminding me that she is human like me, and invite me into her journey. Instead of holding her up as a saint to admire, her writings instead portray an ordinary person simply trying to walk the road of following Christ. In documenting this continual journey, Dorothy Day ended up talking constantly about struggle and cultural isolation. As she writes in her autobiography, *The Long Loneliness,* "We have all known the long loneliness and we have learned that the only solution is love and that love comes with community."

Community is a buzzword these days, primarily for people who don't quite understand how taxing true interdependence can be. As someone impatient with platitudes, I have always been drawn to Dorothy Day's kind of community. I was electrified by the way she wrote about the poor and the suffering and the proper response of the Christian (self-sacrificial love). And I was challenged by the example set by her houses of hospitality, where the homeless and desperate could stay and people could live and work side by side.

One of Dorothy's rules of life was to seek the face of Christ in the poor.

Robert Coles remembers how, the first time he met Dorothy, she was chatting with an intoxicated older woman. She looked up and saw Coles waiting and asked him, "Were you waiting to talk to one of us?" Already quite famous, she didn't assume Coles wanted to talk to her more than he might want to talk to her neighbor. With that simple question, Coles says, "she cut through layers of self-importance, a lifetime of bourgeois privilege, and scraped the hard bone of pride" (*Dorothy Day: A Radical Devotion,* xviii*).* Dorothy Day had absorbed the beliefs of her beloved Christ so deeply that she truly lived as if everyone was of equal importance in a world that applauds hierarchy and prestige.

I am not Catholic, and yet Dorothy Day's attitude to faith has impacted me greatly. I grew up in a conservative church that emphasized personal piety and correct doctrine, but at some point those no longer seemed sufficient as guidelines for life lived in community. Living and working with refugees, the challenges that the poor face soon overwhelmed me – they were the splash of cold water that woke me from my stupor. It was then that I discovered Dorothy Day's books, and she became a guide into a wild new world of following Christ on a downwardly mobile path.

And oh, would I need some wisdom and guidance for that journey! For years I had been too busy "working for the Lord" to spend much time learning from others, especially others who were different from me. I'm a doer. I like to get my hands and feet in the mess of the world. This, I'll admit, is why the writings of Dorothy Day reached out and grabbed me initially. I identified with her iron will and the practical ways she strove to meet the real and tangible needs of those affected by poverty and war.

What made her such a radical? Was it the kerchief she wore in her hair? Her intense writing style? Her involvement in politics while refusing to be conscripted into any political party? Was it her lack of material possessions or her firm belief in the inherent dignity of all people? Or her commitment to the church despite her differences and disappointments? I thought it was a combination of all of these things when I first discovered Dorothy in my early twenties. Now, over a decade later, I have a different answer: her radicalness stems from the transformative love of Christ she experienced throughout her very long and sometimes very lonely life.

Wherever she turned, Dorothy saw Christ

up on his cross. One of her rules of life was to seek the face of Christ in the poor. She found him there, and in so many other places. Christ was the person in line for soup and bread; Christ was the drunk woman having the same conversation over and over again; Christ was the enemy combatant; Christ was the priest she disagreed with; Christ was the young person begging for spiritual direction; Christ was in every reader she wrote for, including me, including you.

Dorothy Day's eyes were first opened to the inequalities of our world when she saw the long lines of people waiting for bread during the Great Depression. Mine were opened the day I realized my refugee neighbors had only been given eight months of assistance by the government and were now expected to be assimilated as fully-functioning members of society. For non-literate, tribal, rural, Muslim Africans plopped down in the middle of Portland, this was ludicrous at best and heartbreaking in reality. I was nineteen years old and dove headfirst into helping these refugee families navigate life in America. I moved into their community and tried to hitch my life to theirs. I ran homework clubs and art classes and English classes. I asked churches and friends and family members to get involved. But life moved on. Volunteers stopped showing up. People weren't as grateful as I had hoped they would be. Countless hours in waiting rooms and on hold trying to navigate bureaucracies did not feel exactly radical. I tried to help everyone as best as I could, but I was failing miserably.

"She is one of our many failures," writes Dorothy Day in a letter to a friend, referencing a woman who left the house of hospitality, most likely to more drink and chaos. Life in community with broken people will always include such disappointments. But they can be met with resilience, and with a faith in the eternal significance of a life lived with the suffering. Such a life will never be easy or tidy; the work is endless and will always stretch on before us.

So how do we go forward? If I am honest, at first I was a bit impatient with Dorothy Day's writings. "Where is the work?" I thought. "Where are all the inspiring stories of her interactions with the poor, the causes of equality that she championed, her countercultural lifestyle choices?" I was, and remain, hungry to hear stories of God's kingdom coming at the margins of society; I want first-person accounts of the glories and heartbreaks at the frontlines. But in Dorothy Day we find someone who at first blush does not seem all that radical. Instead, she is a woman who reads the Scripture constantly, prays, goes to church, partakes in the sacraments, bakes bread and mops floors, writes letters to her friends. She seems very pious, very devout. She comes across as a borderline mystic, sometimes even a bit ethereal, someone who uses religious imagery constantly.

But we know how entrenched her life was in the lives of the very people Jesus said would be blessed – the poor, the sick, the sad, the oppressed – and her spiritual reflections reflect that reality. They spring up from a place of love, not distance. Dorothy Day was not just a radical at the frontlines, writing screeds and organizing protests (although she did all that too). She was a woman bound to daily service in community, deeply committed to rhythms of prayer, reflection, and solitude. She was someone who wanted to live for Christ her entire life, and so she dedicated hers to growing in awareness and understanding of the love of Jesus.

It still astonishes me that it can be this simple and yet so hard to obey.

It still astonishes me that it can be this simple and yet so hard to obey. The love of Christ is everything. Not the work, not the needs, not the good intentions. It is entering into the wound of love of Christ on the cross, and being transformed by it. Dorothy writes: "How can we ever give up thinking and longing for love, talking of it, preparing ourselves for it, reading of it, studying about it? It is really a great faith in love that never dies." Her "work" was her relationship with Christ.

This should cause us to question ourselves. Why am I exhausted by mothering small children while trying to create places of welcome in my neighborhood? Why have so many of my friends who have worked hard to bring justice into the world also faltered, their light dimmed after a few short years? How many other would-be disciples could say the same? What is it we truly want for this one life we are given? A frustrated life of service where we drag ourselves along by the bootstraps? Or a sustainable life that is constantly renewed by the inexhaustible love of Christ and our connection to him?

Dorothy Day invites us into the latter. She calls on us to lay down our burdens and instead link arms with other Christ-followers throughout the centuries. The famous images show her fierce and strong and often alone, but in reality she was connected to a great number of saints – through her books and her prayers and her interactions with her neighbors. Here she found the strength to move forward until the very last moment. She did not view herself as an individual, or a radical, or a prophet; she was one of a great many people whom Christ loved. And like a gorgeous, broken vessel, she was filled with that love day after day and spilled it out wherever she went.

Even now the cares of the world weigh on me. The suffering of people is real and devastating, especially for immigrants, refugees, people of color, and those who are not valued as productive citizens. I am surrounded by these people, and here I sit with three coats hanging up in my closet, wondering at what I am to do.

And yet even now, I know. I will pray for faith, and for love, and for peace. I will fight to carve out space in my life for Christ above all else, to be in community with him and the ones he loves. I still long to be like Dorothy Day, but not in the ways I used to. I don't want to be radical anymore; instead I long to be sustainable, to remain steadfast. I want to walk faithfully in the direction of my Lord, and I don't want to stop until my very last breath. As Dorothy writes, "Our arms are linked – we try to be neighbors of his, and to speak up for his principles. That's a lifetime's job." ⮝

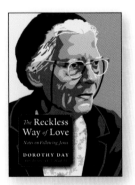

The Reckless Way of Love
Notes on Following Jesus
Dorothy Day
How do you follow Jesus without burning out?

Day offers hard-earned wisdom and practical advice gained through decades of seeking to know Jesus and to follow his example and teachings in her own life.

softcover, 144 pages
Plough, March 2017

**plough.com/
dorothyday**

Unlike larger collections and biographies, which cover her radical views, exceptional deeds, and amazing life story, this book focuses on a more personal dimension: Where did she receive strength to stay true to her God-given calling despite her own doubts and inadequacies and the demands of an activist life? What was the unquenchable wellspring of her deep faith and her love for humanity?

INSIGHTS *on* COURAGE

Teresa of Avila God does not deny himself to anyone who perseveres. Little by little, he will measure out the courage sufficient to attain this victory. I say "courage" because there are so many things the devil puts in the minds of beginners to prevent them from actually starting out on this path. For he knows the damage that will be done to him in losing not only that one soul but many others. If beginners, with the assistance of God, struggle to reach the summit of perfection, I believe they will never go to heaven alone; they will always lead many people along after them.

Taisia Afonina, *Still Life with Pussy-Willows*

Mother Teresa Do not think that love, in order to be genuine, has to be extraordinary. What we need is to love without getting tired. How does a lamp burn? By the continuous input of small drops of oil. If the drops of oil run out, the light of the lamp will cease, and the Bridegroom will say, "I do not know you." My sisters, what are these drops of oil in our lamps? They are the small things of daily life: faithfulness, punctuality, small words of kindness, a thought for others, our way of being silent, of looking, of speaking, and of acting. These are the true drops of love. Be faithful in small things because it is in them that your strength lies.

George Bernard Shaw This is the true joy in life, the being used for a purpose recognized by yourself as a mighty one; the being a force of nature instead of a feverish,

selfish little clod of ailments and grievances complaining that the world will not devote itself to making you happy.

I am of the opinion that my life belongs to the whole community, and as long as I live it is my privilege to do for it whatever I can.

I want to be thoroughly used up when I die, for the harder I work the more I live. I rejoice in life for its own sake. Life is no "brief candle" for me. It is a sort of splendid torch which I have got hold of for the moment, and I want to make it burn as brightly as possible before handing it on to future generations.

Meister Eckhart As long as we look for some kind of pay for what we do, as long as we want to get something from God in some kind of exchange, we are like the merchants. . . . By all means do all you can in the way of good works, but do so solely for the praise of God. Live as if you did not exist. Expect and ask nothing in return. Then the merchant inside you will be driven out of the temple God has made. Then God alone will dwell there. See! This is how the temple is cleared: when a person thinks only of God and honors him alone. Only such a person is free and genuine. ⤳

Sources: *Teresa of Avila: The Book of Her Life,* ed. Jodi Bilinkoff (Hackett, 2008). *Daily Readings with Mother Teresa,* ed. Teresa De Bertodano (HarperCollins, 1993). George Bernard Shaw, *Man and Superman: A Comedy and a Philosophy* (Constable, 1903). *Meister Eckhart: Selections from His Essential Writings,* ed. Emilie Griffin (HarperSanFrancisco, 2005).

The Art of Courage

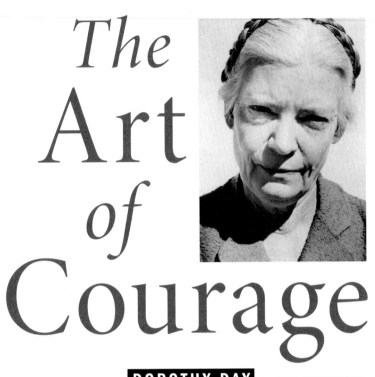

DOROTHY DAY

Learning to Love Recklessly

What does everyday discipleship look like?
Dorothy Day (1897–1980), the cofounder of the
Catholic Worker Movement now being considered
for sainthood by the Vatican, inspired thousands
to follow Jesus' radical way of complete devotion
to God and selfless service to others. In her books,
letters, and diary entries, she lays out what discipleship involves in words that ring true because they
come from a woman who lived them without compromise. The following reflections are taken from
Plough's new book, *The Reckless Way of Love: Notes
on Following Jesus.*

Luca Sartoni, *New York City, December 12, 2015*

Whenever I groan within myself and think how hard it is to keep writing about love in these times of tension and strife, which may at any moment become for us all a time of terror, I think to myself, "What else is the world interested in?" What else do we all want, each one of us, except to love and be loved, in our families, in our work, in all our relationships? God is love. Love casts out fear. Even the most ardent revolutionist, seeking to change the world, to overturn the tables of the money changers, is trying to make a world where it is easier for people to love, to stand in that relationship to each other. We want with all our hearts to love, to be loved. And not just in the family but to look upon all as our mothers, sisters, brothers, children. It is when we love the most intensely and most humanly that we can recognize how tepid is our love for others. The keenness and intensity of love brings with it suffering, of course, but joy too, because it is a foretaste of heaven. ◆

> "What else do we all want, each one of us, except to love and be loved?"

Luca Sartoni, *New York City, December 11, 2015*

"It seems at times we need a blind faith to believe in love at all."

The main thing is never to get discouraged at the slowness of people or results. People may not be articulate or active, but even so, we do not ever know the results, or the effect on souls. That is not for us to know. We can only go ahead and work with happiness at what God sends us to do. ◆

How to draw a picture of the strength of love! It seems at times that we need a blind faith to believe in it at all. There is so much failure all about us. It is so hard to reconcile oneself to such suffering, such long, enduring suffering of body and soul, that the only thing one can do is to stand by and save the dying ones who have given up hope of reaching out for beauty, joy, ease, and pleasure in this life. For all their reaching, they got little of it. To see these things in the light of faith, God's mercy, God's justice! His devouring love! ◆

Luca Sartoni, *New York City, December 9, 2015*

Young people say, "What good can one person do? What is the sense of our small effort?" They cannot see that we must lay one brick at a time, take one step at a time; we can be responsible only for the one action of the present moment. But we can beg for an increase of love in our hearts that will vitalize and transform all our individual actions, and know that God will take them and multiply them, as Jesus multiplied the loaves and fishes. ◆

Do what comes to hand. Whatsoever thy hand finds to do, do it with all thy might. After all, God is with us. It shows too much conceit to trust to ourselves, to be discouraged at what we ourselves can accomplish. It is lacking in faith in God to be discouraged. After all, we are going to proceed with his help. We offer him what we are going to do. If he wishes it to prosper, it will. We must depend solely on him. Work as though everything depended on ourselves, and pray as though everything depended on God. ◆

> "We must lay one brick at a time, take one step at a time."

Luca Sartoni, *New York City, December 8, 2015*

> "The greatest weapon in the world is the reckless spending of ourselves in God's service."

We know how powerless we are, all of us, against the power of wealth and government and industry and science. The powers of this world are overwhelming. Yet it is hoping against hope and believing, in spite of "unbelief," crying by prayer and by sacrifice, daily, small, constant sacrificing of one's own comfort and cravings – these are the things that count. And old as I am, I see how little I have done, how little I have accomplished along these lines. ◆

The solution proposed in the Gospels is that of voluntary poverty and the works of mercy. It is the little way. It is within the power of all. Everybody can begin here and now. . . . We have the greatest weapons in the world, greater than any hydrogen or atom bomb, and they are the weapons of poverty and prayer, fasting and alms, the reckless spending of ourselves in God's service and for his poor. Without poverty we will not have learned love, and love, at the end, is the measure by which we shall be judged. ◆

Luca Sartoni, *New York City, December 9, 2015*

Love and ever more love is the only solution to every problem that comes up. If we love each other enough, we will bear with each other's faults and burdens. If we love enough, we are going to light that fire in the hearts of others. And it is love that will burn out the sins and hatreds that sadden us. It is love that will make us want to do great things for each other. No sacrifice and no suffering will then seem too much. My prayer from day to day is that God will so enlarge my heart that I will see you all, and live with you all, in his love. ◆ ⇢

> "It is love that will burn out the sins and hatreds that sadden us."

Why We Hope

CHRISTOPH FRIEDRICH BLUMHARDT

The Lord Jesus gives us a task on earth: "Watch! – Watch for my coming!" (Matt. 24:42). This is a most important assignment. If we fulfill this task – to watch for Christ's coming – we will find it becoming reality now. When we keep watch, our whole being is directed toward this future. We see it before our eyes, we feel it in our whole life. We cannot be swallowed up by the present, for we are linked to the future; we experience this future already. Our life is renewed again and again and something new develops, something that points the way for us to go: each time it is a glimpse into Jesus Christ's future.

Christ's future is not just one single point in an indefinite period that we are to wait for. If this were true, we would probably all go to sleep while we waited; but his future is already here. This future with Jesus Christ must become the personal experience of everyone, today, tomorrow, and every day. We must be awake to experience how God works through Jesus Christ.

The Savior is coming! He is not quietly sitting somewhere in eternity, waiting for a certain moment when he will suddenly appear. He is on the way. We must always look for him to come among us; we should expect him every day. The coming of the Savior runs like a thread through Christian history, through God's presence in the world. If this thread is to continue we must not give in to sleepiness. The Lord Jesus is coming! There will be times of storm and thunder, of sorrow and suffering; yet in all such storms, all sorrows, and even when we think we cannot go on, there will be new revelations that will enable us to continue working and watching. Then the time will come when our waiting and watching will bear fruit: the Lord Jesus' time will be fulfilled.

Watch, and be joyful. Even though fear overcomes you, watch; the Savior will enter into your life. I have often experienced this. I have been led and I have had to say, "There is a way out of this fear." Even when I felt we could not go on, God showed us a direction – and now we have an inkling of Jesus Christ's future among us. We depend on this coming of the Savior. That we are allowed to expect such great happenings animates our daily life and thinking and will finally lead to victory.

Live constantly in Jesus Christ's future. The Savior himself says, "Of this day and hour no

German pastor and socialist Christoph Friedrich Blumhardt (1842–1919), who influenced Karl Barth and Paul Tillich, preached this sermon on the eve of World War I.

Wayne Forte, *Alarme*

The future we long for is already here.

one knows" (Matt. 24:36). This future of Jesus Christ alleviates the confusion, suffering, temptation, and hostility in the world. Now we have hope. Right now there are large circles of people who hope for a new, free, and good life. They do not think that things will just go on and on, and that humanity will not reach any goal. Now new doors are being opened for the good to flourish, and many people want to take part in serving and helping the need of their neighbors. In great hope, dedication, and faithfulness, even worldly people take part in this task, and in this way are part of Christ's

future. Any hope for improvement, any belief that better days will come for humankind, any striving toward better times, is a proof and a result of this hope that we Christians firmly express by the words, "The Savior is coming!"

We must be alert and watchful. Jesus Christ's future has to become your personal experience. Whenever you experience protection and remarkable help, whenever you are led on new ways and see others being led on new ways, you should think, "This is a piece of Jesus Christ's future." A new wind is blowing in his future. All kinds of signs and proofs of

God's help are visible. However poor we may be, however weak we may feel, we will continue to hope and watch. A time will come when we will be allowed to participate in Jesus Christ's future....

The Savior is coming! He is on the way to you, to me, to us all, in all circumstances of our lives. Even when things are as they were in Noah's time, even if the whole world is apparently concerned with nothing but earthly things, with eating and drinking, with marrying and giving in marriage, we should not give up. We must be a living testimony at all times. Our Christianity must be alive. Our Christian faith must be a light of hope, a light in the midst of people's indifference. It must be a light even in the midst of all the activity of the world. We look forward to greater things than new machines and inventions. We hope for a change to the good in our hearts and in our lives. We hope for the overcoming of the powers of evil, of all sin that still prevails. We expect victory over all the misery that binds so many people, over all the evil and hostile powers that torment humanity. This is our expectation.

Because of this expectation we will not become weary. We will not become forlorn, nor will we become irritable or quarrelsome. We will not be dissatisfied with our conditions and with the events that surround us. In all things we will see the Savior coming. This will surpass by far any apparent triumphs that people experience through their own works. . . .

The future of Jesus Christ must become a reality in world history, in the history of Christianity, and in every Christian's life. Your life must be a piece of Jesus Christ's future – your life and also your death. Our dying should not lead into death but into life. Even in our last moments Jesus Christ's future must touch us.

The dying must say, "The Savior is coming!" The sinners, upon their awakening and repenting, must say, "The Savior is coming!" In all our afflictions we should say, "The Savior is coming!" We must be convinced that all our troubles and afflictions have something to teach us.

In this way we should be watching. I know of no other way to do it. We have to experience his coming. There is justification in thinking that the Savior is quite near. It is right to say with the apostles, "He is at hand, he will come soon!" He will not only come at some moment that lies in a distant future. Our whole life is filled with the coming of the Lord Jesus. Daily we rejoice at his coming. Daily he opens up new ways for us, so we can carry on joyfully. Daily he opens new doors for us; he helps us and protects us, often without our knowledge. Again and again we are allowed to recognize his help when suddenly, like a miracle, we see that we have been protected. This is the Lord Jesus.

Watch and pray, the Lord Jesus is coming! This watching is a part of our life, of our service to God. The Savior seriously urges us to watch, watch, watch! He wants to lay a foundation for it in our hearts, in our whole lives. It is as though he were always waiting and asking: How can I come closer to this person, to that person? How can I meet this one who is waiting for me? How can I go to meet many at a time, so that again and again new victories are given? What can I do to make the call heard throughout Christendom, throughout the whole world, "Jesus lives, Jesus is victor!"?

When we watch we are not thinking of our own lives only. We are watching for the whole world. We are thinking of the world, which is still in darkness. We lift our hearts and heads, saying, "Father in heaven, the world is yours. You have given us minds and hearts with which to wait and strive forward. You have made men and women of us, you who are the God of all gods, the Savior of all humankind."

In the small circle of a family, of a household, we keep watch. Each one, keep watch! Do not fall into darkness and indifference, but watch! Your own hour will come – be prepared for it. The hour will come for your inner growth, for the renewal of your life, and for your death. Watch! Never lose heart. The Savior often comes in the most difficult hour, in the unhappiest times. Watch, for the Savior is on the way!

Watch for the world too. Do not give the world up as though it were lost for all eternity. It is true that Jesus Christ's future brings separation. The fact is that one person can come to faith and to the joy in God while another remains outside for the time being; this should not trouble us. The future of Jesus Christ is and will be a great and powerful help in all situations for all people. All eyes will be opened. We will not be able to say anymore, "This one will be accepted and that one not." People will weep and wail when they see how wrong they were. Their tears are part of Jesus Christ's future, of the Savior's coming, and many will receive help. Thanks and praise be to God!

We cannot say that the Savior has not come, that we have experienced nothing of his future. We live in his future. Just think how much we have been given – how many times we have received help and protection, often very suddenly and unexpectedly. All of a sudden it was here, this future of our Lord Jesus Christ. Let it live among us now! Don't just look to the distant future, as though something impossible would come eventually. Let it come to life now, in our daily life. Let it come to life in your personal experiences. Let it come to life on your sickbed. For the Savior

We expect victory over all the misery that binds so many people.

also comes to the sick, to the poor, to those who have to struggle for their daily bread. The Savior is coming! This certainty is our joy; it is the source of our Christian life. Let it fill our days, today, tomorrow, and every day of our life. This joyful certainty will carry us through all our needs. The fact that we are allowed to say, "The Savior is coming!" is like a surging tide of God's spirit. This tide will never end; it will continue to carry us forward, and bless us in all our thoughts and endeavors, in our whole life.

Therefore watch! Watch, all of you! Let each one be a fighter for Jesus Christ, a servant of the Savior. Surrender your lives and hearts. Be prepared! Jesus Christ will come to you, into your house, into your hearts, into your lives. Never forget this: the Savior is coming! ⤳

Source: Sermon on Matthew 24:36–42 on November 13, 1913, in Christoph Blumhardt and His Message, ed. Robert Lejeune, trans. Plough (1963). To get this classic volume, which includes Blumhardt's biography, as a free ebook, visit plough.com/cfblumhardt.

T. S. Eliot's "Little Gidding"

A Visual Interpretation

ARTWORK BY JULIAN PETERS

Published in September 1942 as the final poem of T. S. Eliot's *Four Quartets,* "Little Gidding" was completed after the poet survived the bombing of London in the Blitz. In this poetry comic by Julian Peters, which illustrates the poem's final stanzas, images of aerial combat and burning churches reference these air raids.

Inspired by a visit to Little Gidding, the site of an Anglican religious community established by Nicholas Ferrar in 1625, Eliot's poem portrays the choice he saw facing humanity: to be destroyed in the fires of war or to allow that fire to purify and restore – through God's mercy and the fire of the Holy Spirit.

> The dove descending breaks the air
> With flame of incandescent terror
> Of which the tongues declare
> The one discharge from sin and error.
> The only hope, or else despair
>   Lies in the choice of pyre or pyre—
>   To be redeemed from fire by fire.
>
> Who then devised the torment? Love.
> Love is the unfamiliar Name
> Behind the hands that wove
> The intolerable shirt of flame
> Which human power cannot remove.
>   We only live, only suspire
>   Consumed by either fire or fire.

What drew Eliot to Little Gidding? Three centuries earlier, after a catastrophic crash of the Ferrar family's mercantile empire, about forty men, women, and children of the extended family left behind a worldly life to devote themselves to godly living, constructive work, and a daily rhythm of Bible study and prayer. The community ran a school, provided lodging for several needy elderly women, and dispensed soup and medicine to the local people.

Even the defeated King Charles I, a family friend, sought refuge at Little Gidding during the English Civil War. (The community found him safer lodgings nearby.) With England once more at war, Eliot wrote, "I think, again, of this place, / And of people, not wholly commendable / . . . / United in the strife which divided them." Though the community faltered after the death of its founders, perhaps something had been won for all time in that place, which continues to attract pilgrims to this day. It is to them Eliot writes:

> You are not here to verify,
> Instruct yourself, or inform curiosity
> Or carry report. You are here to kneel
> Where prayer has been valid.

Are we willing to be purged by the suffering of our age? If so, the poem offers words of assurance borrowed from the fourteenth-century mystic Julian of Norwich: "All shall be well, and / All manner of thing shall be well." ➤

The Editors

Julian Peters is an illustrator and comic book artist living in Montreal. julianpeterscomics.com

WE SHALL NOT CEASE FROM EXPLORATION

AND THE END OF ALL OUR EXPLORING

WILL BE TO ARRIVE WHERE WE STARTED

AND KNOW THE PLACE FOR THE FIRST TIME.

THROUGH THE UNKNOWN, REMEMBERED GATE

WHEN THE LAST OF EARTH LEFT TO DISCOVER

IS THAT WHICH WAS THE BEGINNING;

AT THE SOURCE OF THE LONGEST RIVER

THE VOICE OF THE HIDDEN WATERFALL

AND THE CHILDREN IN THE APPLE TREE

NOT KNOWN, BECAUSE NOT LOOKED FOR

BUT HEARD,

HALF-HEARD,

BETWEEN TWO WAVES OF THE SEA.

IN THE STILLNESS

QUICK NOW, HERE, NOW, ALWAYS—
A CONDITION OF COMPLETE SIMPLICITY

(COSTING NOT LESS THAN EVERYTHING)

The Need of Refugees

FROM OUR DECEMBER 1938 ISSUE

ASHTON KEYNES, ENGLAND. Every day the Cotswold Bruderhof receives by post urgent requests from non-Aryans, who have either already left Germany, Austria, or Italy, or who will have to leave almost immediately because they have been deprived of their means of livelihood. We are publishing a few extracts from letters received, to show our friends the urgency of most of these cases.

In October the Cotswold Bruderhof had already taken in ten non-Aryan immigrants from Vienna, but now their numbers have increased to twenty. Our houses, cottages, and temporary buildings are absolutely full, and it is impossible for us to take in any more, apart from five or six children of parents who are either killed or in concentration camps, or otherwise incapable of keeping their children. We are in urgent need of addresses of people who could give shelter to refugees, even for a short time. Would anyone who is able to give hospitality to one or more of these unfortunate and suffering people write to us at once, and state clearly what kind of accommodation he can offer, and what kind of people he would be able to accommodate, and for how long? In a few months' time we could take in about ten to twenty more refugees, and especially children, provided we can get enough money for building and equipment. Those who feel urged to help, after the shocking persecution in Germany during the last few weeks, but who are unable to offer accommodation themselves, could do a great deal by sending a donation to the Secretary of the Cotswold Bruderhof, Ashton Keynes, Wiltshire; for there is plenty of work and a real opportunity for useful service in this community for those who are so sadly deprived of their means of existence or of making use of their abilities for the common benefit.

With regard to the children, the Cotswold Bruderhof is suggesting a scheme of adoption. A child, with expenses for school clothing, full board, and lodging, costs us about £4 per month. Anyone who wishes to adopt a child by taking over financial responsibility up to that amount should write to the Headmaster, The Bruderhof School, Ashton Keynes, Wiltshire. . . .

We feel most concern about the children, and want especially to open our houses to them as soon as we have enough room, because they are the future, they are innocent, and their suffering is the greatest wrong of all. Nothing, therefore, can give greater joy than to take a few children out from a life of dreadful misery and a hopeless future, and to receive them into a happy community where they can be taught the principles of love, peace, and justice so that later on their energies can be diverted into useful channels for the common benefit of mankind.

Will anyone whose heart is stabbed by the awful misery of non-Aryan refugees, or of those persecuted because of their principles, or of the children, either give shelter to one or two himself or do his best to make it possible for us to welcome more of those who are living in such tragic circumstances? THE EDITOR ✒

Lotte Berger, a Jewish girl from Vienna, was one of the refugee children from the *Kindertransport* taken into the Cotswold Bruderhof in England in 1939.

Listening to
SILENCE

Martin Scorsese's film adaptation of Shusaku Endo's
novel is magnificent and harrowing – and leaves us
with more questions than answers.

SAM HINE

SILENCE. Could this possibly be God's answer to our most desperate prayers? Did God really hide his face as thousands of Christian martyrs were tortured to death?

I'd read Shusaku Endo's novel *Silence* twice before watching Martin Scorsese's recent film adaptation. Any skepticism about Hollywood's ability to do justice to the story soon evaporated. The film is majestic and deeply disturbing in the same way the book is, with the potential to stir deep questions of doubt, faith, and forgiveness in a far larger audience. This historically grounded tale of religious persecution probes the core of what it means to follow Jesus, even more deeply than the glorious accounts of early Christian and Reformation-era martyrdom on which I was raised.

Jesuit priest Sebastian Rodrigues is ready to give his life for Christ and the church's missionary endeavor in seventeenth-century Japan, where brutal persecution has driven the faith underground. To escape death and torture, Christians can prove their renunciation of

Christ only by stepping on his face. The *fumi-e,* the bronze relief sculptures used for this purpose, are worn smooth with the trampling of many thousands of feet.

The worn *fumi-e* graphically illustrates a fact that has held true in every age: for every heroic martyr who holds firm to the end, there are others who apostatize under duress, often repeatedly. The strong – the Japanese peasant Mokichi bound to a cross in the sea, who dies singing hymns after days of water torture in the surf, and missionary priest Garrpe, who throws himself into the sea to rescue his parishioners or die with them – are promised paradise. But what of the weak? Scorsese manages to evoke sympathy for even the despicable character Kichijiro, a stinking, drunken weakling who repeatedly denies his Lord and betrays his fellow Christians, only to return groveling for forgiveness and reacceptance. Had he not been born into a time of persecution, Kichijiro reminds those of us who have not, he could easily have remained a good Christian to the end.

Rodrigues, the last surviving priest in

the country, is prepared to suffer, but can he withstand the torment his sadistic inquisitor, Inoue, Lord of Chikugo, has in mind for him? The foreign priest is forced to stand by as the Japanese peasants for whom he came are drowned or hung upside down in pits in his stead. They have already apostatized repeatedly, but will not be spared unless he, Rodrigues, denies Christ. Only after a night listening to the moaning of the Christians in the pits does he finally hear Christ speaking clearly to him, urging him to trample, to lay down his martyr's crown, his office and good name, his religion, and possibly even his own salvation to save the lives of others. Rodrigues steps on the *fumi-e*. A cock crows.

Any of us in his place might have done the same. And to be sure, "No one has greater love than this, to lay down one's life for one's friends" (John 15:13). Yet the question lingers: Was that really Jesus speaking? Is that what he would have wanted? It's easy to see the appeal of this Jesus, not only in Japan, a Buddhist culture with a different, more human, conception of the divine, but also in the spiritual-but-not-religious, post-modern West, which prizes ambiguity over certainty, doubt over faith, and the humanity of Jesus over his lordship.

The Jesus we meet in the Gospels is often far less ambiguous: "Whoever denies me before others, I also will deny before my Father in heaven" (Matt. 10:33). So is the apostate still doing Christ's will, even as he – unlike the original Christ-denier, the apostle Peter – goes on to collaborate with the Japanese authorities in the suppression of the faith and takes up a life of relative comfort compared with the Christian peasants he has abandoned? Will we find out when his betrayer, Kichijiro, returns once again on his knees, begging Rodrigues to hear his confession and grant absolution? The fallen priest would like to refuse, but once more Christ breaks his silence, and Rodrigues pronounces forgiveness.

What are we to make of the God who foreknew Peter's denial and Judas's betrayal, the Creator of our own fickle hearts? For Endo and Scorsese show us that we too are Peter and Judas, Rodrigues and Kichijiro, always failing

After wading ashore by night, missionary priests Garrpe (Adam Driver) and Rodrigues (Andrew Garfield) are welcomed by Ichizo (Yoshi Oida), a secretly Christian Japanese fisherman who will be crucified as a result, in the film *Silence*.

to emulate our Lord no matter how doggedly we stumble toward him.

Japanese-American artist Makoto Fujimura, in his 2016 book *Silence and Beauty,* describes the effect *Silence* has had on his journey as an artist and a Christian. He memorably recounts his own first encounter with the worn *fumi-e* in a Tokyo museum, and the day he stood on Martyrs Hill in Nagasaki, where twenty-six Japanese Christians were crucified in 1597 after being marched 480 miles with their noses and ears cut off. The hill overlooks Ground Zero, where in 1945 the United States obliterated one of the leading centers of Christianity in Japan. In an age of proliferating Ground Zeros, Fujimura suggests, *Silence* offers "an antidote to the world of trauma, torture, and religious persecution":

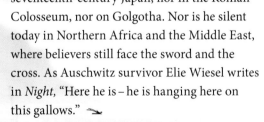

A seventeenth-century *fumi-e*

> When we identify with less than noble characters like Kichijiro . . . or failed priests like Father Rodrigues . . . we are being injected with a vaccine that makes us realize, if we allow ourselves to be honest, that we actually resemble these weak, sometimes comically failed characters. Endo's books expose our true selves. . . . But this awareness can liberate us, Endo suggests, toward compassion, an antidote to a fear-filled world.

Silence may not answer the questions it poses; like much true religious art, it opens us up to the mystery of human frailty and God's justice. All the same, the film remains art, not "what really happened." Under the influence of its beguiling cinematography, we can easily forget that what it presents is at best a partial truth, perhaps even a false choice.

And so something more needs to be said. Over and against Scorsese's vision stands the historical record of the faithful martyrs. On February 5, 1597, when the twenty-six Christians arrived at the Nagasaki hill where their crosses awaited them, one of the youngest, twelve or thirteen years old, reportedly said, "Show me my cross."

For the first two centuries of Christian history, there are many records of martyrs but very few of apostates. (That only changed with the Decian persecution of AD 250, when, threatened with systematic and sadistic torture, thousands of Christians recanted, presenting the early church with a painful dilemma: what forgiveness could be offered remorseful apostates, and how often?) Another parallel can be found in the areas of sixteenth-century Europe where Anabaptism was a capital crime. Of the Anabaptists who were captured and actually faced the death penalty, around half recanted. This is not surprising. What's remarkable is that the other half of them, eventually numbering several thousand, did not. In many cases they – like Mokichi in Scorsese's film, and like many other Christian martyrs of the era, as recounted in Brad Gregory's *Salvation at Stake* – went to their deaths singing.

For me, after watching *Silence,* one thing is all the more certain: God may have been silent at times – perhaps he sometimes even speaks in silence – but he was surely never absent. Not in seventeenth-century Japan, nor in the Roman Colosseum, nor on Golgotha. Nor is he silent today in Northern Africa and the Middle East, where believers still face the sword and the cross. As Auschwitz survivor Elie Wiesel writes in *Night,* "Here he is – he is hanging here on this gallows." ➤

Sam Hine is an editor at Plough.

Editors' Picks

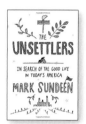

The Unsettlers: In Search of the Good Life in Today's America
Mark Sundeen
(Riverhead Books)

Today many people sense, with varying degrees of urgency, the need to find simpler, more ethical, sustainable, and authentic ways to live. Amid a burgeoning movement of "local food and urban farms, bike co-ops and time banks and tool libraries, permaculture and guerilla gardening, homebirthing and homeschooling and home cooking," Sundeen, author of *The Man Who Quit Money,* goes in search of "more radical, more committed, yet less isolated" exemplars of such a life. His other criteria: they should be raising a family (he'd just married), presumably progressive (like him), not Amish ("you can't join them"), not born rich but bootstrappers, not escapists but working to heal society, and succeeding at a project viable over the long haul.

Sundeen starts with our friends Ethan Hughes and Sarah Wilcox at the Possibility Alliance in Missouri, a petroleum- and electricity-free community dedicated to nonviolent social change (see *Plough* No. 5, Summer 2015). Next he follows Olivia Hubert, a descendant of slaves and a child of inner-city Detroit, as she turns abandoned lots into an urban farm together with her husband Greg Willerer, a child of white suburban punk anarchism. Closer to home, Sundeen finds Luci Brieger and Steve Elliot, pioneers of the local food movement in Montana, successfully raising three children and organic vegetables without compromising their beliefs and values.

The Possibility Alliance community doesn't exist online, yet it attracts over a thousand visitors a year. So why in eight years has only one man joined them full-time? Well, it turns out that, despite the joys, voluntary poverty and simplicity really do mean hardship, self-renunciation, and lots of manual labor. So does sustainable small-scale farming. Most people, like Sundeen, prefer a simplicity that allows for daily hot showers, Wi-Fi, and international travel. That's why the search for the good life remains far more popular than actually living it. Let's hope this book prods at least a few searchers to put down roots.

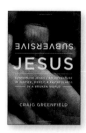

Subversive Jesus: An Adventure in Justice, Mercy, and Faithfulness in a Broken World
Craig Greenfield
(Zondervan)

An eye-opening college break in Cambodia sends New Zealander Craig Greenfield in search of the "real Jesus" who brings good news to the poor. He worries that his desire to "live in a cardboard box" in the slums "might not be such an attractive proposition for a potential spouse" until he meets his match in Nay, a Cambodian immigrant who shares his vision. Together they allow Jesus to upend their notions of family, parenting, charity, hospitality, community, and citizenship.

The tone is breezy, but don't be fooled; Greenfield is in earnest. At times he might gloss over the rough edges of living in community with detoxing drug addicts in a Vancouver ghetto. (He has since moved with his wife and two small children to the slums of Phnom Penh.) And about half way through you'll swear that if Greenfield says "radical," "subversive," or "upside-down kingdom" one more time you'll gag him. But the challenging witness of a family willing to follow Jesus anywhere regardless of the cost is impossible to discount; one hears echoes of Jesus telling a rich young man to sell everything he has, give away the money, and throw in his lot with a homeless leader. People like this give us hope for the world. ⮞ *The Editors*

The Happy Nuns

Learning Joy through Self-Denial from the Sisters of Life

REBEKAH DOMER

Even nuns get a break on Sunday: Sister Mary Elizabeth and Sister Immaculata in lower Manhattan.

What would cause any woman to trade a successful career for a vowed life of poverty, chastity, and obedience? Sister Veronica Mary of the Sisters of Life, a Catholic religious order, puts it this way: "The Christian life is based on love to others, not love to oneself. We have become a world of individuals, a world of people who decide for themselves what is best for me rather than what is best for others. Community life is a declaration that love overcomes the problems that separate people."

Founded in 1991 by John Cardinal O'Connor, the Sisters of Life is an order that is both active and contemplative: they pray but are not cloistered. Their mission is to assist pregnant women in crisis, offering alternatives to abortion. The order has experienced remarkable growth. Just in 2016, fifteen young women from across North America – all younger than thirty-five and all with at least four-year degrees, including four with doctorates – became

Rebekah Domer blogs at bruderhof.com.

postulants. From its small beginning in the Bronx, the order now has eleven locations in the United States and Canada.

Coming from a Christian community myself – I am a member of the Bruderhof – I wanted to learn more about this vibrant fellowship of women, and asked the Sisters for an interview. And so on a frosty November morning, Sister Veronica welcomed me into the Sisters of Life convent in Yonkers, New York. Soon she was telling me her story.

Eileen Sullivan (Sister Veronica's birth name) was the third of six children born to devout Catholic parents in Waterbury, Connecticut. Although her parents had taught her to consider God

Sister Veronica Mary

in all she did, when she started nursing school she began to drift away from her faith. Military recruiters talked her into enlisting. "It wasn't so much the military that I loved but people on a mission together – people with a purpose," she told me. She signed on for three years and was assigned to a nursing job at Andrews Air Force Base in 1985.

After falling in love with a physician, Eileen left the military to join him in Seattle. He eventually proposed. But the fact that he was not a believer forced Eileen to consider her own convictions: "I realized that I had to give my faith precedence. I knew I could never commit my life to someone who did not share the most vital part of me." She broke off the relationship.

Returning home to Connecticut, she worked as a cardiac intensive care nurse for five years. On the job she was confronted with many of the ethical dilemmas associated with modern medicine: "I'll never forget the day I picked up a chart on which a resident had written, 'Please stop food and fluids on this patient.' I thought to myself, 'I can't do that.'" She began to ask herself, "Am I doing what is morally right in my

professional life?" Ever since she had made the decision to put her faith above human love, a restlessness had been growing in her – a hidden sense that there was something more to life than a career, marriage, and material comfort.

On a January day in 1993, Eileen wandered into a church as a priest was delivering a homily that would change her life. The priest spoke about the millions of unborn children being aborted in our country and challenged the congregation to action. Eileen recalled: "Something happened to me at that moment; I walked out of that church thinking, 'I'm going to be doing this for the rest of my life.'"

Searching for a way to respond to the priest's challenge, Eileen came across a pro-life prayer group that, in turn, gave her the phone number for a local crisis pregnancy center. But she didn't call. "Something in me said, 'If I make this phone call, my life is going to change.' I didn't really want that." She had friends and a family that loved her, an interesting job, and a four-bedroom house with walk-in closets full of clothes. "I knew God was calling me, but I wasn't ready."

Still working at the hospital, Eileen read spiritual literature, attended daily Mass, and participated in Bible study groups. At night she went to the chapel. "I remember those nights – just sitting there and feeling such profound peace and yet crying. I asked God, 'What are you doing in my life? Why are you putting these desires in my heart? I don't want to be a nun!'"

She continued to date, but even promising relationships led nowhere. "Nothing seemed to be working out. I longed for love – for a singular love. I began to wonder if there was something wrong with me. I prayed, 'Lord, show me what you want me to do with my love.'"

Sister Jordan Rose paints faces at the Sisters of Life block party, June 2016.

Finally, Eileen called the local crisis pregnancy center and began volunteering. The work soon became her passion.

She was not alone in this. Circumstances had converged in the early 1970s to encourage many men and women to band together to form the pro-life movement in America. *Roe v. Wade*, the landmark Supreme Court ruling of 1973, held that abortion fell within a woman's "right to privacy," and accordingly struck down the law restricting abortion nationwide. This controversial ruling coincided with the advent of ultrasound as a routine tool in prenatal medicine, a technology that revealed the indisputable humanity of the unborn child.

Against this backdrop, the Catholic prelate John O'Connor had emerged with a radical message defending the sanctity of the unborn. On a visit to the Dachau Concentration Camp in 1975, O'Connor had vowed to use his remaining time and strength to uphold the sacredness of human life. Several years later, O'Connor, now a cardinal and archbishop of New York, had put out a call in his weekly newspaper column for women who would embrace a charism of prayer and fasting for the cause of life. Thus it was that the summer

of 1991 saw the formation of a new order, the Sisters of Life.

In 1995, Eileen joined her pro-life colleagues for a retreat in the Bronx that, unbeknownst to her, was sponsored by the fledgling order. As she recalled: "Entering the room, I was met by the young postulants. They had divested themselves of their professional clothes and were wearing an outfit where you all look alike, just the opposite of the world where 'I gotta be me, I gotta have my own signature and mark on the world.'" She met one nun who was a former IBM computer engineer; another had worked in robotics for NASA. "I said to myself, 'Wow! These women are happy – and it seems genuine.'"

It was their joy that drew Eileen to the Sisters. Still, the following four years were tumultuous. "I had to do the great leap of faith from 'A Sister – me? Not even an inkling of a chance,' to 'Wow! Could this be an option?' to 'I need to really think and pray about this,' to 'Wow! I think He's inviting me . . .'"

In September 1999 Eileen took the plunge. She drove with her parents from her home in Connecticut to the St. Frances de Chantal Convent in the Bronx to embark on her postulancy with the order.

"The initial break with my family and friends was extremely difficult," she told me. "It broke my heart to see my mother weeping; we had always been so close. My entire family attended my clothing ceremony that day, and they were all experiencing such grief." Although stricken to be causing her family pain, Eileen had no doubts as she put on the postulant's outfit for the first time. "I was reminded of the scripture that entreats us to 'put on the new self, created after the likeness of God in true righteousness and holiness' (Ephesians 4:24). That day as my family drove away, I felt such joy: 'God, now I can give my heart totally to you!'"

Eileen believed that through her vows of total surrender to God and his service, she was declaring Christ's victory over the materialistic forces of separation and death that threaten to destroy our world. Her new life was confirmed when she took a new name, Sister Veronica Mary of the Divine Mercy, or, more colloquially, Sister Veronica.

Although she now wore a habit, Sister Veronica's spiritual transformation was not finished. "I had to unlearn so many things. Moving from a human perspective to one focused on God took time and patience." But as she struggled to surrender herself entirely, Sister Veronica experienced more and more of the peace that had eluded her earlier. "All of a sudden you live, move, and breathe with this deep conviction that you are part of something greater than yourself. Our joy does not depend on extraneous circumstances. Joy is the weapon that can cut through darkness."

After hearing Eileen's story, I joined the other Sisters for a common meal. Near me sat Mother Agnes Mary Donovan, the order's Superior General. I asked her how she would respond if someone criticized the Sisters for throwing their lives and talents away doing menial tasks such as working in the community laundry when they could be achieving prominence in professional life or curing cancer.

"Our community life is meant to be a witness to the life of love God wants people to live," she replied. "When you look at a community of sisters who are held together by a spiritual bond, it shows people that there is something much deeper to life than what the world offers."

It struck me that although the Sisters' calling involves great sacrifice, it is a living imitation of Christ. For Jesus too, doing God's will required him to lead a nomadic life, going from village to village as the Spirit led, healing the sick, driving out demons, and preaching the good news. He was also led repeatedly into the wilderness for times of prayer and solitude with his Father. Jesus' life was not his own. From his inconspicuous birth among animals to his death between criminals on a cross, he embodied the sacrificial love of God. He knew he had been sent "to do as the Father has commanded me, so that the world may know that I love the Father" (John 14:31).

What does it mean for the rest of us to do as the Father commands us? As Sister Veronica's story illustrates, God works uniquely in each life, leading us to varied expressions of his will. But discipleship of Christ always demands a radical turning from a life of sin – that is, repentance and conversion. As Mother Agnes put it, "We leave those aspects of the world behind that inhibit us from pursuing the living God. We do so very purposely so that we are free to pursue the call from the Lord to live in relationship with him. Our separation from the world is to facilitate living in truth with that call. We need a separation from the worldly aspects of the flesh in order to move more deeply in our relationship with the Lord."

"We need to keep the bar high," another sister at the table added, "and through that, challenge others to respond with their lives to Jesus' call to leave father and mother, home and fields for his sake. In a disobedient world and culture, we are called to show people that things are empty and friendships unsatisfactory unless God is in the picture."

What role, I asked the Sisters, do religious communities such as theirs play in the broader Christian church? "Religious life," one sister answered, "is a foretaste of heaven. Here you have a united people living together in harmony and peace, worshiping the Lord. We remind the church and the world that there is a God, and that he's worth giving up everything for."

Sister Veronica added that in her experience, suffering is inherent to a life of discipleship. "If you love God," she says, "you are willing to suffer for others. This brings us to the key. We live in a world that runs from sacrifice and suffering at all costs. We need to accept the cross in the everyday experiences of life. The richness of life is found in working things out together because it is the love between us that reflects the gospel."

Some might object that such a way of life together is impractical for all but a few monastics. Yet Scripture makes clear that Christ's way is opposed to the values of contemporary culture. To the extent that society is built on the individualistic pursuit of material possessions, prestige, and power at the expense of others, it will be unable to comprehend how a life consecrated wholly to God makes sense. Reflecting on Jesus' words, "What will it profit a man if he gains the whole world and forfeits his soul?" (Matt. 16:26), the English writer J. B. Phillips writes:

> The good life is conceived almost entirely in terms of creature comforts, labor-saving appliances, better clothes, better and longer holidays, more money to spend, and more

leisure to enjoy. . . . None of these things is wrong in itself. But when they are assumed to satisfy every desire, ambition, and aspiration of man, we are surely right to be alarmed at the grip of materialism. For when possessions, pleasures, and the thought of physical security fill a man's horizon, he ceases to ask himself such basic questions as "What am I?" or "What am I here for?"

It is not that we moderns, in our addiction to materialism, have asked for too much – rather, it is that we have been satisfied with too little.

It was this dissatisfaction to which Eileen responded by becoming Sister Veronica. For her, this meant embracing a way of life that is fully human. Reflecting on her first encounter with the Sisters, Eileen recalled, "These women were young; they wanted to change the world, and they were doing it through joy!"

How is it with us who claim to be followers of Christ? Are we standing out as the "light on a hill" that Jesus speaks of in the Sermon on the Mount? Are we the "yeast" that permeates the dough with kingdom values? Do we uphold the uncompromising way of Christ that leads to eternal life for those who are willing to sell all they possess to acquire the pearl of great price?

To be sure, not everyone is called to be a priest, monk, or nun, or (for that matter) to be a member of the Bruderhof. But it's equally true that none of us who claim to be followers of Jesus is let off the hook. Christ calls each of us to follow him completely, and it is he, not we, who determines where and how we are to serve. If we accept his call wholeheartedly, the joy that shines out from the faces of the Sisters of Life will be ours as well. ⤚

Learn more about the Sisters of Life and read their stories at sistersoflife.org.

(Continued from page 8)
spending a lot of time in his stories, and these portray a much more multifaceted view of rural life than Murphy's essay would lead one to believe. . . . Port William's past is riven with violence, anger, and sin, yet it also carries love, forgiveness, and beauty. . . . [His characters'] search for redemption sounds a lot like the gospel to me.

Jeffrey Bilbro, at Front Porch Republic

Tamara Hill Murphy responds: I wholeheartedly agree that Wendell Berry's fiction expresses important aspects of the gospel, as Jeffrey Bilbro writes, and I honor him for this. Nonetheless, his fictional characters resist the sort of full transformation that comes only by way of repentance. To say this does not diminish the truths that Mr. Berry's stories do portray, including those identified by Jim Severance. Rather, it's to point out that, in these works, a piece of the gospel is missing. This gap need not trouble scholarly critics reading the works purely as literature. But it does matter greatly to those of us twenty-first-century Christians who are seeking to practice aspects of Mr. Berry's vision in our own lives. We must recognize the dissonance between the ideal of community held up in the Port Williams stories and the kind of community that is wholly formed by discipleship of Jesus Christ. To those among my Christian friends who look to Berry's writing for a model of how to cultivate good, true, and beautiful economies, I'm urging appreciation but also discernment. The gospel is greater than even the best ideals.

Punk Plough

On Jason Landsel's "Forerunners: Joe Strummer": This just brought tears to my eyes. I only subscribed to *Plough* recently, and I've already found some insights that have helped me be a better pastor, but someone writing about my musical hero Joe Strummer?! – Naw, that couldn't happen here. I miss Joe to this day, and every Thursday night on my radio show I always play at least one Joe tune. He would have been mighty proud to be included here.   *Tim Christensen, Butte, MT*

Thank you for your continued, excellent work with *Plough*. I was especially thrilled to see the Joe Strummer piece. It opened multiple conversations with non-believers here in Portland regarding a timelessly prophetic Christianity, which is open, strong, and so needed in our time. Your work helped me bear witness in a very cynical place.   *Paul J. Pastor, Bridal Veil, OR*

Take It or Leave It

I cancelled my *Plough* subscription after two issues because I live a very simple, God-centered life – no television, phone, computer – all of that "stuff." Both issues of *Plough* brought to mind new evils I had never heard of and really didn't need to know. (Yes, there were truths woven in, here and there.) So, with sadness, I cancelled.

Mary Burt, Canton, CT

Thank you so much for another very thoughtful magazine. I congratulate you on the variety and independent thinking of many of your articles, representing all shades of opinion from many different perspectives and faiths. It is rare to receive a magazine without obvious bias. Please keep up the good work.

June Curtis, Nottingham, UK

We welcome letters to the editor. Letters and web comments may be edited for length and clarity, and may be published in any medium. Letters should be sent with the writer's name and address to letters@plough.com. ⤸

Traudl Wallbrecher, 1923–2016

BERNHARD KOCH

Shocked to the core by the Holocaust, in 1948 a young woman began her lifelong search for a living, authentic church. She would go on to cofound a Catholic community inspired by the first church as described in the New Testament. Here is her story.

Gertraud "Traudl" Wallbrecher was nine years old when Hitler rose to power in her native Germany, and sixteen when World War II began. As the leader of a Catholic Youth Movement group of girls, she experienced firsthand the terrors of dictatorship, risking her life in the underground resistance. At the same time, she saw how many churchgoing Christians succumbed to Hitler's ideology out of fear, opportunism, or conviction.

Drafted into military service in a hospital near Munich in 1945, she was brought face to face with the horrifying extent of Nazi brutality when she witnessed the evacuation of the Dachau concentration camp. For the rest of her life, the horror she had seen kept her asking: "How could this crime – especially the mass murder of my Jewish fellow citizens – have happened in a country that is so thoroughly Christian? Why wasn't the church strong enough to mount an effective resistance?"

After the war, Wallbrecher hoped that the restoration of civil liberties, including religious freedom, would be accompanied by a wave of deep-going repentance and revival. Yet that is not what happened. Instead, she watched as an unprecedented, silent exodus from the church began – a process of de-Christianization whose contours are only now becoming clear.

Dr. Bernhard Koch is a member of the Integrierte Gemeinde and its Community of Priests.

Traudl Wallbrecher with then-Cardinal Ratzinger and Johann Christoph Arnold, senior pastor of the Bruderhof communities, at a 1995 meeting at the Integrierte Gemeinde's Villa Cavaletti community near Rome

Wallbrecher sought to respond in a way that was not just theoretical but practical. At that time she met a young man, Herbert Wallbrecher, who shared her background in the Catholic Youth Movement and also her questions. What should church life look like in the aftermath of the war and the Holocaust, which had called every value into question? The two were drawn together in their seeking and married in 1949.

From the very start, the young family became a magnet for like-minded believers searching for a new expression of church life. In theologian Hans Urs von Balthasar's afterword to Paul Claudel's play *The Satin Slipper,* the group found a question they felt to be the key challenge: "How is it possible to live completely in the world, yet in full obedience to God?" Through their study of liturgy and with new methods of biblical interpretation, the group realized that the original life of the church had been, quite simply, community. For example, it was to church communities sharing a common life (*koinonia*) that the apostle Paul addressed his letters. In fact, these were the communal churches in which the texts that we now know as the New Testament first took shape.

Would it be possible to pick up the thread of New Testament–style community after so many intervening centuries? No, on the one hand: today's spiritual, cultural, and social conditions are far too distant from those of the biblical world. Yes, on the other hand: because the church is still, at its heart, a community – one that is open to all believers, not just clergy and monastics.

On the basis of this conviction, an ambitious and unpredictable experiment began. People of diverse backgrounds, ages, and professions joined together in a common life; in many cases they literally lived together, worked together, and pooled their income.

The Integrierte Gemeinde and the Bruderhof are sister communities, one Catholic and the other Anabaptist, that are both inspired by the early church. At this historic meeting convened by Wallbrecher, Cardinal Ratzinger and Pastor Arnold together read aloud accounts of the martyrdom of sixteenth-century Anabaptists at the hands of Catholic rulers. Ratzinger then remarked:

> What is truly moving in these stories is the depth of faith [of these men], their being deeply anchored in our Lord Jesus Christ, and their joy in this fact, a joy that is stronger than death. We are distressed, of course, by the fact that the church was so closely linked with the powers of the world that she was able to deliver other Christians to be executed because of their beliefs. This should be a deep challenge to us, how much we all need to repent again and again, and how much the church must renounce worldly principles and standards in order to accept the truth as the only standard, to look to Christ, not to torture others but to go the way of witnessing ourselves, a way that the world will always oppose, a way that will always lead to some form of martyrdom. . . .
>
> It is important [to realize] that we cannot bring about unity in the church by diplomatic maneuvers. The result would only be a diplomatic structure based on human principles. Instead, we must open ourselves more and more to [Christ]. The unity he brings about is the only true unity. Anything else is a political construction, which is as transitory as all political constructions are. This is the more difficult way, for in political maneuvers people themselves are active and believe they can achieve something. We must wait on the Lord, that he will give us unity – and of course we must go to meet him by cleansing our hearts. ➤

Their communal life also found its expression in liturgical celebrations. The apostle Paul's picture of the body of Christ as being one body with many different members inspired the new community's name. Borrowing a word popular in the 1960s, they named themselves the Integrierte Gemeinde (Integrated Community). In 1978, the new movement was officially recognized by its local bishops, one of whom was Joseph Cardinal Ratzinger.

For Wallbrecher, a special passion was building bridges to faith for people who had lost their connection to the church. In her view, this would require a convincing and fresh manifestation of church life that was not bound to received traditions. She found inspiration in the works of modern authors and filmmakers as well as in other communities, such as the kibbutzim in Israel, which she visited repeatedly. In all this, her goal was a way of life as appealing as the city on the hill and the light of the world. Holding fast to the biblical promise that God always wants to "make all things new," her efforts anticipated what the Catholic Church would later refer to as "the new evangelization."

Pope Benedict XVI, who has been the community's friend and mentor over the decades, summed up the essence of Wallbrecher's life when he wrote to her in 2008:

> The flame that you ignited in 1948 has not been extinguished. The fire of the Holy Spirit burns away much that is human, yet ignites a light that spreads its warmth even beyond the bounds of time, since it comes from God's spirit. May the quiet flame of your community always feed on the greater communal flame of the Church's faith and thus become one of the fiery tongues by which the Holy Spirit speaks in this world.

Traudl Wallbrecher died in July last year; her husband Herbert had preceded her in 1997. She leaves behind a church community that still strives to live "completely in the world, yet in full obedience to God." ⤳

To learn more about the Catholic Integrated Community (Katholische Integrierte Gemeinde), visit cic-online.org. *This article is a translation by Erna Albertz of "Gott schafft immer Neues," in* Theologica *No. 3 (Katholische Integrierte Gemeinde, 2016).*

What Is Church Community?

TRAUDL WALLBRECHER

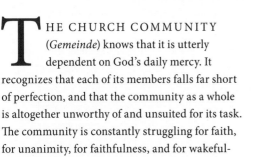

THE CHURCH COMMUNITY (*Gemeinde*) knows that it is utterly dependent on God's daily mercy. It recognizes that each of its members falls far short of perfection, and that the community as a whole is altogether unworthy of and unsuited for its task. The community is constantly struggling for faith, for unanimity, for faithfulness, and for wakefulness. Threatened from within and from without, it survives only thanks to God's care. I know, of course, that the universal Church's heroes and saints are stationed elsewhere – and yet the community has a duty to speak of how God is at work within its own small fellowship.

The church community . . . must show the surrounding world that even today all areas of life can find their liberation within the kingdom of God. Through its unanimity, it can demonstrate that human beings are able to live together in peace.

From a letter to Joseph Cardinal Ratzinger, 1983

(Continued from page 80)

Müntzer believed in God's power to speak through visions and foretold the imminent collapse of the current world order. Along with fellow visionaries, he founded a missionary church and zealously spread the message that, as written in Revelation, God now wanted to raise up a chosen people, leading them into epic battle that would result in a new society without poverty or private property.

Persecution followed their reformatory efforts, and Müntzer's life turned itinerant as he was expelled from one town after the next. Along the way he married Ottilie von Gersen, a former nun. During his travels he set up printing presses and distributed his pamphlets to anyone who would read them, particularly the lower classes, whose support for him grew. Deadly riots and attacks on churches, castles, and monasteries raged throughout Germany. Growing more incendiary, Müntzer saw himself as the "prophet of terror called by God" to bring violence against the evil ones. As he shifted from religious reformer to full-blown radical, a rift widened between him and Luther, whom he now considered a hypocritical "Wittenberg pope." In another sermon he referred to Luther as "Brother Fattening-pig." In response, Luther aligned himself with the rulers Müntzer opposed, urging them to crush the zealot and his followers.

Hearing about the increase of violent flare-ups, Swiss Anabaptist reformer Conrad Grebel and others in Zurich wrote to Müntzer, pleading for the populist leader to adhere purely to Christ's example:

> The Gospel and its adherents are not to be protected by the sword, nor are they to protect themselves. . . . True Christian believers are sheep among wolves, sheep for the slaughter; they must be baptized in anguish and affliction, tribulation, persecution, suffering, and death. . . . Neither do they use worldly sword or war, since all killing has ceased with them – unless, indeed, we should still be of the old law. And even there (in the Old Testament), so far as we can recall, war was a misfortune after they had once conquered the Promised Land. No more of this.

Sadly, such counsel went unheeded, and the calamitous slaughter at Frankenhausen was the end result. Müntzer implored the peasants in his final letter, written from his prison cell:

> Flee from the shedding of blood. You definitely must not suffer such defeats as that of Frankenhausen. Without doubt each one seeking his own selfish interest more than the justification of Christendom caused this defeat. Against this I now warn you faithfully: you must not give in to rebellion again, so that no more innocent blood may be shed.

Under torture prior to his execution, Müntzer called out, *"Omnia sunt communia"* (all things in common), still envisioning a world with distribution according to each person's need. His vision became reality in the communal life of brotherhood that grew out of the Anabaptist Reformation in 1527. The Hutterites and other Moravian Anabaptists shared everything in common as outlined in Jesus' teachings, not founding their life through violence but through repentance and believer's baptism. As summarized in Peter Riedemann's *Hutterite Confession of Faith,* "From each according to his ability, to each according to his needs."

Müntzer's example had made clear the terrible cost of promoting the kingdom of God through violence, yet it was in these pacifist communities, in which brotherly and sisterly love was not just a word but an economic and social reality, that the heart of his vision was realized. ⤳

Müntzer referred to Martin Luther as "Brother Fattening-pig."

Thomas Müntzer

JASON LANDSEL

Frankenhausen, Germany, May 15, 1525. The slaughter lasted only minutes. One moment, the throng of several thousand armed peasants, till now so often divided into rival factions, was united in singing an expectant prayer: "*Veni, creator Spiritus!* – Come, Creator Spirit." The next, the air was suddenly heavy with smoke and screams under a barrage of cannon fire. Many fled; many others were left groaning and limbless, gasping questions toward the sky. Blood from the fallen seeped into the battlefield, now covered with the boot prints of the six thousand mercenaries, or *Landsknechte*, fighting in the armies of Philip I of Hesse and Duke George of Saxony. Better equipped than the disordered peasant army, they had massacred the enemy.

> **Fight the fight of the Lord! It is high time!"**
>
> **Thomas Müntzer**

Thomas Müntzer had inflamed this rebel army with talk of prophetic warfare:

> God promised that he would help the afflicted, and such a promise is valid for us. The princes are truly tyrants. . . . God will not tolerate this any longer. He wants to annihilate them. Look at the sky. See the sign of his grace, the rainbow! God is showing that he is supporting us, proclaiming the defeat and destruction of our tyrannical enemies!

Now their rainbow, which had appeared just before the battle began, had vanished. For days it had brought the peasant armies hope: God's signal to his elect ensuring that with prayers and pitchforks they would soon sweep the threshing floor clean. The hour of vengeance was at hand, they believed, and God's judgment was on its way.

But God didn't descend that day in Frankenhausen. Only six of the princes' army fell or were wounded, while peasant casualties numbered in the thousands. Their shattered barricade, made of chains and farm wagons, along with makeshift weapons, lay abandoned as surviving peasants fled, leaving their pure white banner trampled and spattered with gore. Many who tried to escape were hunted down and executed on the spot. Müntzer himself was soon captured, hiding in a farmhouse and still clutching his bag of writings, giving him away as one of the leaders of the rebellion. At the hands of the conquering princes he was detained, examined, and tortured. On May 27, humiliated and broken, he was beheaded.

Who was this man who, five hundred years later, remains one of the most formidable, and also one of the most controversial, voices of the early German Reformation? Born in 1490 in the Harz Mountains of Germany, Müntzer received a decent education, studied theology, and became a Catholic priest. Soon, however, he began to question what he saw as the greed of the clergy and their extravagant lifestyles that came at the expense of desperately poor peasants. Attracted to Martin Luther's ideas, he collaborated with him regarding the posting of Luther's ninety-five theses. As Müntzer aligned himself more fully with Luther's reforms, he began to preach openly against the unjust distribution of wealth.

(Continued on preceding page)

Jason Landsel is the artist for Plough's *"Forerunners" series, including the painting opposite.*